Issei and Nisei
The Internment Years

Issei and Nisei

The Internment Years

Daisuke Kitagawa

THE SEABURY PRESS · NEW YORK

To My Wife and Children
Fujiko and Karen and John

Preface

The year 1967 marks the 25th anniversary of the mass evacuation of Japanese Americans, both Issei and Nisei, from the Military Zone A on the West Coast. In that evacuation I was caught up along with 110,000 other men, women, and children. It was at once an intensely personal and extensively corporate experience for all involved.

In this book I have attempted to share with my readers that experience—my personal experience within the context of the corporate experience of Japanese Americans as a whole in their forced internment years: 1942-44. The book is *autobiographical*, but it is not my autobiography. If anything, it is a collective autobiography of the Japanese-American community as a whole, in which I am simultaneously an observer, an actor, and the narrator. The result is that I am describing the Japanese-American community from within, as one of its members, but I am not in any sense whatsoever speaking for all the others who are equally its members. The point of view or the perspective from which observation is made is strictly my own. What is presented in the following pages, therefore, is not a history, but a portrait of an ethnic community of which I am a part sketched against its historical background. The reader will notice that in everything described I am involved and that everything described has been seen through my eyes.

The original manuscript when finished turned out to be nearly twice as long as a book of this sort should reasonably be. Consequently, no small number of materials of general interest and historical value had to be omitted. A good number of personal names have been retained for the express purpose of paying tribute to these people for the significant parts they played in making my life richer in those trying days. Names of many more should have been added, but space did not permit. To them—and they are by no means nameless to me—I want to pay my tribute.

This book could not have been written had it not been for two men. The late Mr. Lewis Palen, whom I chanced to meet in Geneva, Switzerland, in 1956 encouraged me to start writing it; and Mr. Arthur Buckley, of The Seabury Press, urged me to finish it. I am particularly indebted to Mr. Buckley for his many valuable editorial suggestions.

D.K.

Leonia, N.J.
May, 1967

Contents

Issei and Nisei
The Internment Years

Introduction:
Day of Decision

In the fall of 1939, I became resident minister of St. Paul's Church, a small mission among Japanese truck gardeners on the outskirts of Kent, in the White River Valley between Seattle and Tacoma, Washington. The majority of Japanese in the Valley were staunch Buddhists, and my tiny mission had had rough going for a number of years. Actually, I was attached to St. Peter's Church, the Japanese mission in Seattle itself, which had a Japanese priest in charge. I was to help him with his youth program, in addition to my resident duties in the Valley. At both missions Deaconess Margaret Peppers gave me invaluable assistance.

When I arrived in Seattle, I had been in the United States for two years as a student at General Theological Seminary, New York City. I had come directly from Fukui, Japan, where I had been engaged in pastoral work for four years. (In 1945, a little short of a month before Japan's surrender, my mother was killed in a U.S. raid on Fukui.)

Having come to General Theological Seminary in order to become better equipped to be a future leader of the Christian Church in Japan, I concentrated exclusively on my

theological studies while in New York. Once, however, I was
persuaded to give a talk to a group of young people at one
of the Japanese churches in the city. It was a pleasant surprise to find myself facing a good-sized audience of keen-
looking young Japanese men and women. Because it had
never occurred to me that Japanese people might not understand the language of Tokyo and Yokohama, I merrily proceeded to speak for a good half hour in eloquent Japanese.
At the end of my address it was a rude awakening to discover
that my pearls of wisdom had been cast in vain—no one had
understood me. That incident gives a good indication of my
naïveté then about the problems of Japanese Americans, not
to speak of the race problem in the United States.

Seattle and White River Valley

That was my first surprise; others soon followed. I shall
never forget my first day in Seattle. The number of Japanese
men working as porters at the railroad station astonished me.
When I reached Jackson Street, the scene before me was utterly unreal. How could this be an American city, I asked
myself, with so many Japanese stores and Japanese people
all about? And the first "cottage meeting" at the home of a
member of my Valley mission carried me right back to the
cottage meetings in the country town in Japan where I grew
up. Could these men and women have been in the United
States since 1924, as they must have been? At the reception
held for me by the church people, Japanese men and women
proudly told me in their welcoming addresses how long they
had been in the United States—twenty-five, thirty-five, even
fifty years. My turn came to respond, and I did so in English,
because I could not believe that anyone could live that long
in this country without mastering the language. When I sat
down, everyone applauded—not for what I said, but out of
politeness. Gently, an elder informed me that to be understood by the older Japanese, who had been born in Japan
and were commonly referred to as "Issei," I would have to
use Japanese.

I had much to learn—and quickly. The teenagers were my charge, and what a charge they were! Most of them were "Nisei," that is, Japanese who were born in this country of parents who had come from Japan.

The congregation of St. Paul's Mission was an unusual one in that it was made up of a handful of Issei and a majority of Nisei, of whom a majority were high school and grade school children. In 1939 there were scarcely a handful of married couples among the Nisei.

With few exceptions, Japanese families in the White River Valley were farmers. The daughters of these families, by and large, upon graduation from local high schools went to Seattle to work in white people's homes, not so much as domestic servants or maids, but as something like "in-service trainees" to be homemakers. Early in June every year most of the girls working in Seattle returned to the Valley for the summer, to work on their parents' farms. One Sunday in 1940 I was stunned to see the little chapel filled with somewhat citified girls, and commented, "I know summer is here, for flies and girls are back with us!" As for the boys, most of them stayed on the farm; few went to college.

My ministry consisted largely of my being around, and not much more. I used to spend a good deal of time visiting with the young people on the farms and getting acquainted with their parents, who were almost all Buddhists. Those were infinitely less complicated days, and they were infinitely less sophisticated people. Regardless of their family religion, I was, for all practical purposes, the village parson.

From the fall of 1939 to the spring of 1942, there was not one funeral service at St. Paul's Mission. Young people were just beginning to get married. Until the war in the Pacific hit us, we enjoyed a peaceful, almost idyllic, rural community life. And I cannot help admiring those Issei who were Buddhist and who so gladly entrusted their children to the care of the Christian Church, as represented by an American deaconess and a young upstart of a clergyman who had so recently come from Japan.

I had been cordially received into the diocese of Olympia by the clergy, and soon I began to take part in its programs for young people—summer camps, conferences, forums, and so on. The young people rapidly accepted me as one of their clergy, as my fellow clergy in the diocese already had. In fact, I soon found myself living in three worlds: that of the Issei, that of the Nisei, and that of the diocese. It was a glorious period of my life.

I did not forget, however, that in two years I was to return to Japan to serve the church there. That was why I had come to the United States in the first place. As a result of that assumption, I made a serious study of the position of the Issei and the Nisei in America. I was so curious about American society and the American people that I paid little attention to the racial discrimination imposed upon Japanese Americans. As a minister, I generally was fully accepted into the Christian fellowship of the American people. When others sometimes spoke of racial discrimination, it seemed to me an academic matter.

Strange as it may sound now, I did not feel then that being a Japanese was in any way a handicap. To be sure, had I, with my name and my physical characteristics, had to look for a job, I would have very soon found out differently. To be sure, what Japan had been doing since 1932, and more especially since 1937, did not make it easy for me to keep my head up among my American friends. Even so, I did not feel ashamed of being Japanese. It took me time to realize that Nisei were not a little ashamed of being children of Japanese parents. At first, when I became aware of it, I could not understand why that had to be.

December 7, 1941

On the fateful day of December 7, 1941, I had, as usual, an early service at St. Paul's, Kent, and then drove to Seattle for the late service at St. Peter's. As I read the Prayer for the Whole State of Christ's Church, I was moved to insert the names of President Roosevelt, Secretary of State Stimson, and the special Japanese envoys, Nomura and Kurusu, praying God's special guidance upon them as they tried to avert a shooting war between the two nations. I mention this because I seldom did this sort of thing in a service; but on that morning I was moved to do it. After the service I was a dinner guest of Dr. and Mrs. Paul Shigaya in Seattle. Immediately after dinner we learned that Japan had made a surprise attack on Pearl Harbor.

Instantly I decided to go back to the Valley, for in Seattle there were, besides my senior priest, the Rev. Gennosuke Shoji, several Japanese clergymen of other denominations. Furthermore, city people could help themselves much more efficiently than country folk could. In the Valley I was the only Japanese clergyman, and if I were ever to be of real service to those farmers, this was the time.

On arrival, I went directly to Fred Meadowcroft, a vestryman of St. James's parish, Kent. Speechless, we looked at each other for a few seconds. It is no small thing to be bound by such a tie of fellowship that at a time of crisis no spoken word is needed to understand exactly what is in another's mind. We immediately went to see the mayor and the chief of police, to let them know of my availability, as a Christian minister, for whatever service might be required to keep that biracial community at peace. We were advised to see the chairman of the town's Civilian Defense Committee, a lumber dealer who was virtually a stranger to me. The remarkable thing was, as I now look back, that each of the men I saw that afternoon took me into his confidence with no hesitation whatsoever. I am fully convinced that my unshakeable faith in the American people has its roots in that afternoon's experience.

One task had to be done quickly—the cancellation of the big annual party planned for that evening by the Japanese community. I had several key men of the community inform everybody of the cancellation. The Valley was calm that night. When I went to bed, the day's occurrences seemed more like a dream than reality.

Next morning, however, the reality was inescapable. I was awakened by a telephone call from Deaconess Peppers, who told me that a number of the Japanese community leaders in Seattle had been picked up during the night by FBI agents. This was inevitable, and even routine from the standpoint of the government, but it was a terrible blow to the Japanese community, one that left everyone utterly dismayed.

What can one person do under such circumstances? From that moment on, my life ceased to be my own, for I was thrown into the task of being a friend to hundreds of Japanese families in the area, and at the same time serving as liaison officer between the Japanese community and the rest of society. No one authorized me to act as such, but somehow I was driven to feel that this twofold task had been thrust upon me.

1   Condemned to Be Aliens:
The Issei

From the standpoint of the Japanese-American community, the disaster of Pearl Harbor happened at the worst possible time—although no time would have been good, I hasten to add—because their community was in an exceedingly vulnerable position. In order for the reader to understand how vulnerable that community was and the scope of the disaster that overtook it, it will be necessary to sketch something of the history and background of the Japanese in America.

At the time of the attack on Pearl Harbor, Japanese Americans were roughly divided between the Issei (literally, "first generation"), approaching retirement age, and the Nisei ("second generation"), who were not yet much beyond adolescence. The two missions I was serving represented, with respect to age distribution, a good cross section of the general Japanese community. Among the Issei we did not have a single man less than fifty or a woman less than forty. Among the Nisei, on the other hand, most were in the fifteen-to-twenty age group. The number of Nisei children in grade school was conspicuously small; and not a single child of Nisei parents had reached kindergarten. Most of the youth attended junior and senior high school or college. A few college graduates were just beginning to become economically independent, and only a handful of Nisei were married. This was the peculiar pattern of age distribution, and one did not have to search far in order to find the reason for it.

The Oriental Exclusion Act of 1924

The Oriental Exclusion Act of 1924 completely and abruptly stopped the flow of immigrants from Asia into the United States. Any newcomers, such as ministers, teachers, treaty merchants, or students, were allowed only temporary admittance; permanent residence was out of the question. Under the Exclusion Act, Asians were accounted unassimilable into American life and were, therefore, branded as aliens ineligible for naturalization. This conclusion, of course, was not reached by scientific research or proved by actual experience. It was a myth fabricated for a specific purpose.

Those who supported the Exclusion Act argued that the Japanese and other Asians could never become Americanized, and they pointed to the language barrier. Now it is true that scarcely an Issei spoke decent English, although they had been in the country at least fifteen years. On the other hand, despite almost daily attendance, during their grade school and high school days, at the special schools maintained by the Japanese community, the Nisei could not speak halfway decent Japanese. People used to say that the Japanese were by nature poor linguists, and the Japanese themselves believed it. The fact of the matter was that this language block was not a racial characteristic, but existed for sociopsychological and cultural reasons. Indeed, it was, at first, in no small part due to racial prejudice and discrimination, and later became a lasting consequence of the Exclusion Act.

The Act had many far-reaching effects. After its passage,

thirteen western states enacted Anti-Alien Land Laws, which prohibited "aliens ineligible for naturalization" from owning or operating real estate. These laws prevented Asians who had come to the United States prior to the Exclusion Act from taking root in American society and, perchance, being fully assimilated, while the Exclusion Act cut off further Asian immigration.

The Japanese community felt these blows immediately. No Issei could now legally own his home, his farm, hotel, grocery store, or business establishment. True, some Japanese managed to save money in the bank accounts of their children and to purchase a farm or business in the name of their children, having themselves legally designated as guardian. When the children, the legal owners, attained their majority, the status of the parent then became that of tenant or employee; and thus parents continued to live on the farm or operate the business. The state authorities accepted the practice and the legal profession condoned it, probably because these children born in the United States of alien parents had the right, on attaining their majority, to choose either United States citizenship or that of their parents' nation. Potentially, however, these children were aliens, too, since they had yet to make their choice. Prior to 1941, no one had seriously raised that question.

The Japanese Immigrant

After the Russo-Japanese War of 1904-1905, the leaders of Japan were preoccupied with but one idea—how they could most efficiently modernize their country. To them the answer lay in Westernization. But only a small minority of Japanese were growing rich and powerful; this development was largely at the expense of the masses. Under these circumstances, thousands of young men eagerly looked for better economic opportunities elsewhere. The call for cheap labor, first from Hawaii and later from the state of California, was, therefore, a God-sent opportunity, and a wave of emigration swept the country. Tens of thousands left Japan for America, the land of opportunity.

The Japanese, when he left Japan, had a most positive attitude toward America. Whatever the official government policy on emigration might have been, the emigrant regarded America as his land of opportunity, where he could finally make a man of himself. He came to America filled with dreams. He was fully prepared to undergo any degree of hardship and to discard Japanese customs and manners if that would help him realize his dreams. He had no aversion at all to returning to Japan, in two years or ten, as a completely Americanized gentleman. He was certain that his countrymen would look up to him as a hero if he returned to his homeland fully Americanized.

The Japanese was enthusiastically welcomed both in Hawaii and in California—as a source of cheap labor. So long as he remained cheap labor—a human machine, as it were—he continued to be welcome. When he began to show more than casual signs that he was not forever going to be cheap labor and to indicate that he would assert his economic independence, self-respect, and human dignity, the anti-Japanese propaganda started. All sorts of derogatory and discriminatory action based on race began. Life for the Japanese immigrant was thus made exceedingly difficult and painful, with psychological agony as well as physical hardships.

Terrible though this social ostracism was to him, the Japanese took it on the chin. He was determined to make a success of himself. He even accepted racial discrimination as a price he had to pay in order to be fully Westernized. To the Japanese of that period, and to those who came later, there was nothing worthy of pride in Japanese culture, whereas there was nothing to be deprecated in Western civilization. In this frame of mind, it was not very difficult for Japanese to accept prejudice and discrimination practiced by the Westerner. (Prejudice and discrimination shown against the Japanese by the Chinese or the Korean was quite another matter!) This acquiescence was not due to the so-called philosophical attitude on the part of the Japanese but, rather, to his basic attitude toward Western civilization and toward his own culture.

After he had lived and worked in the United States for several years, the Japanese immigrant found himself continuing to admire America as a dreamland which he might some day make his own. Physically he was in America, working for Americans and resting his hopes for his future in America; and yet socially (and psychologically) he was apart from the American people. He was in America but not of America. The Japanese community came to be an insulated cultural island in American society, not by choice but as a result of rejection and social ostracism by American society.

The emphasis then came to be laid on being accepted. In a word, the Japanese yielded to the American terms under which he was to be accepted, and developed a rather peculiar idea of his relationship to American society. This idea, founded upon his gross misconception of American society and its attitude toward him, played a series of psychological tricks on him then and later.

First and foremost, he was made keenly conscious of the radical difference that existed between the Japanese way of life and the American way. His method of dealing with that difference was to discard his own way and take up the way of the American people, whom he keenly desired to resemble. That, of course, is humanly impossible, but the Japanese in America found himself boxed into a psychological corner. The result was that the Japanese community, as I found it in 1937, was still far from Americanized, yet far behind contemporary Japan; it was not accepted by the American and no longer acceptable to the Japanese back home. Thus there began a pattern of segregation which, paradoxically enough, kept the individual Japanese in America from becoming completely disintegrated.

All this happened long before the word *apartheid* appeared in the vocabulary of human relations. From the vantage point of a later day, I can now see quite clearly what an ethnically segregated community in American society means. The Japanese-American community in 1940 made that abundantly plain.

The Japanese community was also extremely static—like a bear cooped up in a cage. Not in any sense a dying community, it had, however, a great deal of energy that it had little opportunity to expend. And it is amazing—little short of miraculous—how little hostility was to be found among the Japanese toward the American society which had been keeping them in this position for such a long time. No amount of discrimination discouraged them from trying to win acceptance. The individual Japanese concluded that it was not unnatural, not even unjust, for Americans to reject him as long as he was not like them. How he wished, for example, to be able to speak English perfectly, without any Japanese accent! How he wished that he had been taller and better built or of lighter complexion, so that they could not so easily tell that he was a Japanese! Because of his eagerness to be like an American, he came to minimize and discredit his own cultural heritage. Without knowing it, he was a victim of what psychoanalysts call self-hate, which is all the more poisonous because its victim usually is not aware of it.

The Language Problem

The problem of language was a particularly nagging one. Because of his uncritical admiration for America and his neurotic desire to be able to speak English like an American, the Issei was overwhelmed by the tremendous difficulty of the English language—which no one can deny—and could not bring himself to speak it unless he could do so perfectly. Knowing that he could not possibly do so, he felt ashamed, and was afraid to open his mouth.

In the second place, the racial ghetto in which he had

been confined made it practically unnecessary for him to master English. He lived among his own countrymen with a persistent, though increasingly faint, hope that some day he might be allowed to cross the gulf surrounding his community. For all practical purposes, his life in America was nothing but a continuation of his life in Japan. He continued to hope to reach America long after he had arrived.

Both psychologically and sociologically, English had not become a tool to be used in his daily life. Psychologically, it was an end in itself, a symbol of his having become like an American. Sociologically, his segregation offered little occasion for him to need English to communicate his ideas. No social intercourse, no communication of ideas. No participation in the national life—social, political, or economic—no concern for what was going on in the nation. The total frame of reference of the immigrant Japanese in America had thus been reduced to his own tight little community.

In the meantime, he was not looking back to Japan. The only sense in which Japan was his frame of reference was as the place to which, in the remote future, he would like to retire. Consequently, he became more and more oblivious to what was going on in his homeland. Nationalistic politicians back in Japan might have thought of the Japanese immigrants in America as Japan's outpost, but the immigrant himself had no such idea. He had left Japan only to improve his own economic state, or in order to avoid the military service, or because he was disgusted with the way the "little folk" had been maltreated in the name of national security and advancement. He had no desire to be used by the Japan he left behind him.

The distance between the Japanese community in America and Japan in the 1930's revealed itself most conspicuously in the historical dimension. I have already mentioned the first prayer meeting I attended in the White River Valley. It was very much like the prayer meetings I used to attend, as a small boy, in my father's parish in a little country

town in Japan. Little had I dreamed of finding anything like
them in the United States. But there these people were, not
one of them having changed even a little from the day he left
Japan around the turn of the century. The racial prejudice
and discrimination in American society had pushed them
back into segregated communities that invariably were nothing but reproductions of the Japan they had left. Japan, of
course, kept on moving, changing for better or for worse.
Consequently, each year the sociocultural distance between
the actual Japan and the Japan in the memory of the immigrant Japanese in America grew wider and wider. I knew
instantly when I first came in contact with him that the immigrant could no longer fit into contemporary Japan. From
the point of view of contemporary Japan, the Japanese in
America was an extrahistorical, if not anachronistic, being.

The Issei Community

This situation inevitably resulted in, among other things,
a poverty of ideas among the Japanese in America. The Japanese community was not participating in the ongoing life of
either America or Japan. Such being the case, there was little
possibility that any new ideas would emerge. The Japanese
in America was exclusively preoccupied with the cold business of making a living and raising his family, trading and
associating almost exclusively with his fellow countrymen.
His community could not escape becoming ingrown.

Father Shoji, the old priest in charge of St. Peter's Mission,
Seattle, used to tell me all sorts of stories about the early days
of the Japanese community in Seattle. He, of course, knew
the whole story. There were many, many things which, as I
heard them, almost made my heart stop or my hair stand on
end. I mention this simply to indicate that, by the time I
arrived, the Japanese community was already extremely
tame, decent, and orderly. On the surface it was peaceful and
economically not too badly off, but internally it was quite
neurotic.

There were present two symptoms of collective neurosis. The first was the divisiveness of the community, which could be seen at various levels of its life. In fact, it gave the impression of being a community split into innumerable factions or, better, a conglomeration of many unrelated small groups. Cooperation was most difficult to achieve. In order to have a majority of people participate in a community enterprise, some measure of coercion couched in terms of a carefully worked out scheme of social censure, such as playing upon one's desire to maintain status in the eyes of the group, had to be used. Contrary to the commonly accepted myth that Japanese stick together or are clannish, the reality, as I found it, was an extreme divisiveness.

Obviously, no one can live by himself. The profoundly human need for social intercourse and fellowship was met by the many small groups. The characteristic common to all those organizations, whether religious or social, recreational or semipolitical, was that the membership qualification was predetermined for each individual. An example is the *kenjinkai*, or prefectural club. After nearly half a century on this side of the Pacific, one would expect that not even the Japanese would be so conscious of their native places, at least as an important precondition for friendship. But the contrary was true. Wherever there were two or three from the same *ken* (prefecture), they formed their *kenjinkai*. No one from another *ken* could belong to it; no one from the same *ken* could avoid it. Once organized, the *kenjinkai* could, and did, perform some useful functions, but whatever good it might have done was outweighed by its contribution to community divisiveness. This was, from another perspective, a carryover of the modern version of the primitive tribalism which had not quite died out in Japan even a century after the Meiji restoration. This ethnic communalism protected individuals from becoming completely disintegrated in competitive society and, at the same time, prevented them from attaining the individuation necessary for life in a democratic society.

Under the system, one did not need to choose friends in whom trust could be placed; they were predetermined for one on the basis of *ken*. The institution of the "picture bride," by which a great majority of the immigrant Japanese were married, contributed to the perpetuation and intensification of the *kenjinkai*, which in turn became a link between the new world and the old.

In addition to the *kenjinkai*, churches also provided a basis for communal groupings. Christians and Buddhists had little to do with each other. Each religion had several denominations, and one's denominational affiliation went far in determining one's social circle. In the case of the Buddhist, his denominational membership had been carried over from the old country and to a great extent coincided with the membership in the *kenjinkai*. In the case of the Christians, most of whom were converted after they came to America, their denomination was due largely to accident. Consequently, in each denominational group there were people from many different prefectures of Japan. As social groups, therefore, there developed a rather marked difference between a Christian congregation and a Buddhist one. The latter was strictly a "closed" and homogeneous local group, little different from what it would have been in the old country; the former had an element of heterogeneity and openness.

In general, groups were organized with the primary intention of serving others. That is to say, all the groups that existed in the Japanese community were inverted, drawing a circle around their respective memberships and restricting sociability to the group while sharply defining the member's attitude toward those inside and those outside the circle. Friendliness was obligatory within; indifference was normal without.

The saving factor was that almost everybody belonged to more than one group; thus, the innumerable small circles overlapped one another, and the community appeared to be multidimensional and multibonded, and not simply an aggregate of unrelated small groups. But a careful analysis made it quite clear that, with the possible exception of Christian congregations, all the social groups among the Japanese were of the kind that emphasized the intensification of the solidarity within the circle. This caused not a little intergroup tension within the apparently unified community and gave it all the characteristics of a split personality.

The second symptom of community neurosis was seen in the attitude common among the Japanese in America toward other racial groups, including the Caucasians. The internally split Japanese community suddenly became a unified community the moment it was made conscious of the existence of other groups. The one over-all organization of the Japanese was the *Nihonjinkai* (Japanese Club), which was, in its primary intention, a social rather than a political organization. Its importance for the Japanese, however, was most keenly felt only when the Japanese community faced a crisis. Under normal circumstances, everybody was preoccupied with his own affairs and paid little attention to the *Nihonjinkai*. But when the Japanese became the target of racial discrimination or when goods from the home country were boycotted in America, thus intensifying anti-Japanese sentiment, the *Nihonjinkai* received enthusiastic support. This inevitably gave the impression to an outsider that it was a political organization through and through. Actually, it simply became the accepted channel of communication of the Japanese people with the organized bodies outside, be they the American government, the Japanese government, the local chamber of commerce, or what have you, although it must also be admitted that within the *Nihonjinkai* itself there was constantly a lot of petty politicking among the various factions of the community.

The other lamentable fact was that the Japanese looked down on other minorities in America—the Negro, the Chi-

nese, the Mexican, the Filipino. As he had an irrational
sense of inferiority toward the Caucasian Americans, so he
had an even more irrational sense of superiority toward the
other ethnic or racial minorities. To be sure, he did not go
out to discriminate against them, for he was in no position
to indulge in such luxury. Inwardly, however, he was sure
that he was far superior to all these groups, and resented being lumped together with them. His thought may be aptly
expressed by what one of the most mature Nisei said in
analyzing the Nisei psychology: "I may not be as good as the
white man, but thank God I am not half as bad as these
others." This preposterous attitude of the Japanese must
not be judged morally, but diagnosed psychologically. As
it took an external threat to create internal unity in his
community, so he needed to look down upon other groups
to reassure himself of his value and dignity as a man.

I had one of the shocks of my life when I awoke to this
reality. But that shock was nothing compared to the one I
suffered when I discovered the language in which it was expressed. No group was spared the derogatory adjectives and
nicknames. I felt moral indignation every time I heard a
Japanese use a derogatory expression about other racial
groups, until I finally came to realize its full meaning. I
must admit that it took me quite a few years to do that.

So far I have been discussing the Issei exclusively. Let us
conclude our discussion with a brief statement about his
religious life. Although a vigorous effort had been made by
Christians to convert the immigrant Japanese, and despite
the fact that there was hardly a Japanese who at one time or
another had not received some service or ministry from the
Christian church, the majority remained unconverted. I say
"unconverted" advisedly, because it does not mean that they
were convinced and practicing Buddhists, Shintoists, or anything else. Although there were Buddhist and Shinto
churches and organizations, there was practically no religious

ministry rendered by them, nor was it sought. The Japanese immigrants were not interested in religion at all. They were preoccupied with everyday living. Religion entered the realm of their concern only when it presented itself as a means to help them.

2 Alienated Citizens: The Nisei

In 1940, it was estimated that better than seventy-five per cent of the people of Japanese descent in the United States (not including Hawaii) were Nisei, or "second generation." In the normal American usage of the term, the Nisei is in reality the first-generation American of Japanese descent. The Japanese, however, looked at it from the standpoint of Japan and called the immigrants "first-generation Japanese" and their children "second-generation." Whether this was one of the consequences of the Exclusion Act or one of the precipitating causes, one can hardly be sure. In all probability no one reasoned out the terms before they were adopted. Nevertheless, they do betray the basically ethnocentric character of Japanese mentality. It is not very likely that the immigrant would have forgotten that he was a Japanese, however well he might have been treated; but there can be no doubt whatsoever that the anti-Japanese sentiment prevalent in American society constantly and painfully reminded him that he was nothing but a Japanese, no matter what. On the other hand, the Oriental Exclusion Act and all it implied caused the Nisei to be ashamed of his

ethnic origin. On the surface, the effect upon the Nisei was the exact opposite to that upon the Issei, and the Nisei turned out to be just as knotty and complex a character as the Issei. Moreover, the Issei's conception of the Nisei did not make the problem any simpler.

It was not too difficult, as we have noted, for the Issei to accept his predicament. He was able to see quite clearly the marked difference, in kind if not in degree, between his cultural attainment and the prevailing cultural standard of the white Americans. In typical old Japanese fashion, he could and did say to himself, *Shikataganai!* ("This cannot be helped"). At the same time, he did not passively accept his predicament. The Issei, to a man, seem to have made a vow that for the Nisei the situation would be completely different.

From this, one can readily see how important a place the Nisei came to occupy in the mind of the Issei. Indeed, the Nisei gave positive meaning to the Issei's life. The Issei parents lived simply to see their Nisei sons and daughters grow up into first-rate Americans, so that they could shout from the housetops to all the world, "See, we knew it all the time!" To achieve that, they did not mind paying any conceivable price.

To the Issei, the Nisei was an incarnation of America that had broken through the barriers and had come to live in the midst of the segregated Japanese community. "Flesh of his flesh, bone of his bone," the Nisei was *his* beyond dispute, and yet he was an American, too. The Nisei was there already! The gulf had been bridged. The wall of the partition had begun to crumble. The goal of the Issei's long pilgrimage was now in sight. That which was unreachable had come to him. Indeed, he had not hoped in vain.

The Nisei, however, constituted a threat in the minds of that segment of American society which was imbued with racist ideology. All kinds of measures were devised to treat the Nisei as other than an American citizen. Branding him

as a descendant of "aliens ineligible for naturalization," these racists attempted to misconstrue the state laws so as to exclude him from the public school system and from such normal citizenship rights as owning property and to prevent him from choosing his area of residence or selecting his own mate. With or without law, the employment opportunities for the Nisei were severely limited, so that for all practical purposes he was not much better off than the Issei. In the late 1930's, however, the majority of Nisei were still quite young. The oldest were only beginning to taste the bitterness of racial discrimination against them. Those who were then in college and high school were just becoming aware of the unhappy and painful experiences that the future had in store for them.

The Nisei Dilemma

The Nisei thus found himself caught between the two Americas—the one of his parents' dream and the one in which he was to live. The bitterness of the cup the Nisei had to drink was incomparably worse than that of the Issei because he faced maltreatment by his own country, although in reality he was neither different from nor inferior to his fellow Americans, a fact which he could see quite clearly. The law declared him to be a citizen; he himself had no sense of belonging to any other country; and yet in practice American society treated him as an undesirable alien.

Sooner or later an explosion was bound to come. The Nisei I knew back in the late 1930's and early 1940's was already under terrific tension, a tension that was completely internalized. He was torn between what he thought he was and what others thought he was. In other words, the Nisei found himself in a position where he was compelled to be what he actually was not, fighting against all kinds of images he thought others were forming of him. He could not relax sufficiently to be himself, and was driven from insecurity to insecurity.

I am not a professional psychoanalyst, but a pastor. As a bilingual pastor, I ministered simultaneously to both the Issei and the Nisei, which gave me a unique opportunity to know both. The composite portrait of the Nisei I am about to draw, therefore, is composite in a dual sense, for it is a collective portrait of the Nisei as a group as well as a portrait from three or four different perspectives. When I drew the portrait of the Issei, little was said about the Nisei; but, in drawing a portrait of the Nisei, reference to the Issei is indispensable.

I came to know the Nisei when he was in his adolescence. That, of course, is the period when the tension in the parent-child relationship is at its worst. But the tension I found between the Issei and the Nisei, which the Nisei internalized, was something quite different from the usual tension that exists between the adolescent and his parents.

Of primary importance was the Issei's conception of the Nisei. Because of the Issei's never-fading longing to make America his own, to him anybody who was *of America* was an object of envy. When the Nisei started to go to school, play with the neighborhood children, and use the English language more and more, the Issei felt that his many years' hardship would soon be over, now that his child could speak the language of America as well as any American. This ability to speak English was sufficient to make the Nisei a superior being in the mind of the Issei, who thought that the quicker he could forget Japan, the better off he was going to be, a characteristic that some anthropologists call "cultural amnesia." At the same time, the Issei was psychologically unable to make any constructive, step-by-step effort to achieve his aim. Into this psychopathological situation entered the Nisei—one who unmistakably belonged both to the Issei and to the United States.

During my short ministry I almost never came across an Issei who had taken any practical steps to return to Japan. Almost every Issei was eagerly looking forward to the day

when the Nisei—flesh of his flesh and bone of his bone—
might be established as a citizen and fully vindicate the
cause for which the Issei had sacrificed so much. This in itself was a remarkable and, in a way, pathetic change. Long
before the Nisei reached the age of majority, the Issei had
become dependent upon him. In the culture of Japan, a
son could be anything from a social security card to an old-
age pension for his parents, and in that sense every parent
was eventually dependent upon his child. That cultural
trait accentuated itself in the case of the Issei. He not only
depended upon his son or daughter for support in his old
age, but for much else long before that. For example, only
in the name of his Nisei child could he own real estate. Thus,
his economic independence in America was utterly dependent upon the citizenship of his infant child.

When the Nisei started to go to school, the Japanese community began to have contact with American society. Few
Issei parents participated in PTA activities, but youngsters
made their friends and knew no such thing as racial difference. Gradually the Caucasian children's parents got to
know the Issei people. When Taro and Johnny became
chums, Taro's father ceased to be just a Japanese to Johnny's
father, and Johnny's father simply a white man to Taro's
father. Whatever the law of the land might say about the
Asians as "aliens ineligible for naturalization," these two
men were destined to get to know each other. Little wonder,
then, that the die-hard racists insisted on complete segregation, and not least in the public schools, for to those racists
their own children were the potential saboteurs.

Thus the Issei, through his Nisei children, began to feel
as though he finally belonged in America. At the same time,
his feeling of inferiority toward his children came to influence the parent-child relationship.

The predicament of the Nisei was this: He was destined
not to honor his father and mother. How could he, when
they were so utterly dependent on him? How could he re-

spect them, when they themselves were convinced that he was far superior to them? I saw love and affection abundantly shown by the Nisei toward his parents, but seldom respect. It could not have been otherwise, when the Issei, despite all his native ability and intelligence, his education and training, his cultural attainment and technical skill, was a helpless and unacceptable foreigner insofar as American society was concerned.

The second aspect of Nisei tension grew out of his relation to American society. It had been impressed upon him by his parents and by the Japanese community that he was an American, and he made every effort to prove that he was. But American society apparently thought of him otherwise and treated him as a Japanese, simply because of his face, his parents, and his name. He was subjected to discrimination in boy-girl relations when he reached the later teens, and in job hunting when he graduated from college. It is not surprising, then, that in the late 1930's the Nisei appeared to spend most of his energy trying to convince both himself and the American public that despite his looks and his parents, he was really American.

Many a time I heard the Nisei emphatically answer, "I am American," when asked by a somewhat bewildered Caucasian whether he was Chinese or Japanese. It sounded perfectly silly to me, for while in New York, I had been so used to hearing Americans say, "I'm Irish," "I'm Italian," "I'm English." Was it not perfectly natural in the West, where Japanese, Chinese, and Filipinos were found in such a mixture, that people should ask whether he was Chinese or Japanese? Of course, it is quite possible that some people had in mind the nationality, and others, the race or national origin. Whichever it was, what should it matter? Yet the Nisei found it next to impossible to answer quietly and unassumingly, "I am Japanese." He had to say in no uncertain terms, "No! I am an American." Not infrequently an unsolicited remark was added—as it were, a footnote to document the statement—"I cannot even speak a word of Japanese, you know."

Nisei Defensiveness

Thus we come to the third dimension of the Nisei's internal tension—Japan. Japan and Japanese culture, anything that identified him as Japanese, became taboo to the Nisei, simply because it was detrimental to his trying to establish himself as an American. The only recourse left for him, as far as he could figure out, was to disprove that he was Japanese. All things being equal, if he could convince the American public that despite his physical characteristics and name, he could not speak even a word of Japanese or appreciate Japanese culture, then, he reasoned, they would accept him as an American.

An extraordinary logic, I must say! But it is not too fantastic at that, for there had been, not very many years before, a lot of good and sincere Americans who believed that that was the only way for true Americans to emerge. I refer to those who advocated the amalgamation theory of Americanism. Every immigrant was urged to discard his national culture and heritage as soon after his arrival in the United States as humanly possible and to turn into a colorless American. It was from the point of view of the amalgamation theory that Asians appeared to be utterly unassimilable. Consciously or unconsciously, therefore, the Nisei was trying to prove his Americanism to the advocates of the amalgamation theory in their terms. The Nisei did not invent that logic, neither did he resort to that technique on his own accord, but he did so almost as an instinctive reaction to the hidden irrational logic underlying American social thinking.

However, when the Nisei became self-consciously anti-Japanese, he paradoxically became more Japanese than he needed to be. In his effort to disprove that he was a Japanese, he took his Japanese heritage much more seriously than the average Issei did. It is like the atheist who takes God far more seriously than the average Christian does. And, of course, it was utterly impossible for the Nisei not to be Japanese, no matter how hard he tried. Under more favorable circumstances he would have accepted himself as he was, and made the most of it, so that he would be an American of unique background and distinct potential. If he could have done that, he would have been able to transcend his racial difference. He could also have taken pride in being able to speak Japanese fluently. Indeed, he could have appreciated the culture of Japan and would have wished to introduce it into America.

That the Nisei in his adolescence could not have done it is perfectly obvious. The odds against him were too formidable. In fact and in practice he was in every way a member of the Japanese community, except that his language was English. This irked him not a little; and to counteract it, he turned to an extreme form of Americanism, rejecting everything, with the possible exception of food, which in any way identified him as a Japanese.

Largely because of his youthfulness, the Nisei's eagerness to be fully accepted as an American did not become a movement, in the sense of an organized collective effort on behalf of the whole group. Every Nisei had, deep in his heart, the same burning desire, but few ventured to go out of step with the rest. Very few thought of putting up a legal fight for their citizenship rights. At the same time, if my experience with the Nisei in the subsequent fifteen years is any indication, the Nisei would not have stood up to fight for his rights as an American citizen—that is, fight legally—under normal circumstances, because the Japanese community provided him with a basis of emotional security. Subjectively, he was glad to have a group to which he unquestionably belonged. It was a haven for him from the turbulent voyage through the gale of racial prejudice.

Here we come to the fourth dimension of the Nisei's internal tension: his relationship to his fellow Nisei in the

Japanese community. Being an American, as against being
a Japanese, does not reside in the fact that one cannot speak
the Japanese language or that he cannot appreciate the Japanese arts. If there is anything which characterizes the
American, it is his freedom from every form of communalism—tribal, ethnic, cultural, and religious. To be sure, he
lives in groups and communities; he is not an individualist
who denies social solidarity of any kind—but he *is* a person
to whom his and everybody else's individual personality is
more important than any group. He seeks a genuine human
fellowship with others on the basis of common interest and
common concern, and frequently on no specific basis. I am
not saying that all Americans are like this, but it is safe to
say that America is made up of community builders rather
than of pre-existent communal groups. This is what makes
America unique both as a nation and as a culture.

The Nisei might have bent over backward to be anti-Japanese in many respects, but he had not cut himself loose
from the Japanese community, or even from the ethnic
solidarity that bound him to all other Nisei and Issei. Thus
he did not become so thoroughly Americanized that he might
be ostracized by his fellow Nisei. He was extremely sensitive
to the censure of his community. What others in the community might think of him was extremely important. It
may be said that the Nisei competed surreptitiously among
themselves. But it was a competition to be better than others
within the terms of reference authoritatively set by the community. To upset or to ignore such terms and to dare to be
different from the rest of the Nisei was both intolerable to
the society and unthinkable to the individual.

That, incidentally, was one reason why there was practically no juvenile delinquency in the Nisei community. As
long as one stayed within it, one would know, without being
told, what was acceptable and what was not acceptable to
the community. As a matter of fact, the Nisei was being
governed by the Confucian ethic of propriety, according to

which the crucial issue is not what is right and what is
wrong for one to do under a given circumstance, but what is
acceptable to the community of which one is a member.

When that ethos was transplanted into the midst of American society, it brought about a peculiar consequence. While
the Nisei was at once a member of the Japanese community
and a potential member of American society, his attitude
toward his parents was collectively determined quite inde-
pendently of the merit of each case. A Nisei, in order to be a
respectable member of the Nisei community, had to be re-
bellious against his parents and the Issei in general. This
kind of intergeneration conflict is a universal phenomenon
in all races and cultures. In the case of the Japanese community, the problem was aggravated because the adolescent
Nisei revolted against his parents, not only because they belonged to a bygone generation, but also, and more primarily,
because they were Issei, an alien group. Here the rebellion
took on a complexion of self-hate. In his parents the Nisei
found that element in himself which made it difficult for
him to be accepted by American society. Consequently, regardless of what kind of persons his parents were, one could
not be a Nisei unless he had something approaching a
grudge against them. It was almost his union card for belonging to his circle.

Accordingly, the Nisei as a group were driven to form a
tightly knit community of their own, compulsively defensive
and compulsively aggressive at the same time. Every time I
heard a Nisei emphatically declare that he was an American,
I could not fail to detect the defensive-aggressive state of
his mind. This, of course, was inevitable. Man accepts himself only when he knows that his society has accepted him.
Conversely, society does not find it easy to accept a man who
has not accepted himself. Which comes first? It seems that
society, in the course of history, builds up its ethos or mores
or unwritten codes, and that anyone who cannot fit into that
standardized pattern is categorically rejected, an action

which becomes a stigma for the individual and makes it very hard for him to accept himself.

The state of mind just described is what we call minority psychology. It is usually accompanied by one or more of the following marks: a chip on one's shoulder, a belligerent attitude, the tendency to resort to escape mechanism when faced by a difficult task, petty jealousy among fellow members of the group, inhibitions, and overly sensitive self-consciousness. All these marks, it seems to me, stem from the preoccupation with acceptance by the dominant group. Acceptance of a person in a psychological sense is one thing that cannot be forced. It is not primarily a matter of ethics, but of mental health. But the minority-group members become so preoccupied with how they can be accepted by the majority group that they tend to make an ethical issue of it and try to force the majority group to accept them on the basis that it is the right thing to do. Of course, it is the right thing to do, but racial prejudice has temporarily or partially cost the majority group its sanity, thus making it unable to see the ethical right or wrong in the matter. In such a situation, to treat the problem of acceptance by the majority group as simply an ethical matter and to approach the majority from a purely rational point of view is, paradoxically, a symptom of an irrational state of mind on the part of the minority group.

This is what makes race prejudice so costly to society as a whole, in that both the prejudiced and those who are the target of prejudice lose their sanity when it comes to their attitude toward each other; neither can see the other straight. The minority, however, is bound to get the shorter end, because the majority can afford, or at least thinks it can afford, not to take the minority into account and to treat it as if it did not exist; the minority is made to feel that its existence and well-being depend entirely upon its acceptance by the majority. The majority can have the luxury of accepting the minority on the majority's terms, while the minority cannot

force its own terms upon the majority. The minority, therefore, tends to become desperate in its effort to be accepted
by the majority, a frame of mind that usually makes its
whole situation worse than before.

I previously stated that there was no organized effort by
the Nisei group as a whole to make their real worth known
to the American public. The frantic effort to be accepted
was entirely on an individual basis. A very serious situation
could have developed in the following ten or twenty years,
when the Nisei was entering adulthood and becoming responsible for his living and the support of his family. There
could have developed insidious individual competition
among the Nisei that could easily be manipulated by shrewd
operators in the majority group to their own advantage and
to the Nisei's further economic defeat. As it was, however,
in 1940 the Nisei as a group were a little too young to have
reached that stage. And the war, with the wholesale evacuation, changed the entire situation so completely that it can
almost be said to have served as shock therapy for the collective neurosis of the Nisei community.

Nisei in Uniform

The pathetically ingrown and inwardly divided Japanese
community in America, the atmosphere of which was getting
rather stale, suddenly acquired new vigor when, under the
Selective Service Act, a number of Nisei boys were called to
military service in 1939. The Issei was psychologically prepared to face that eventuality. It was another case of *Shikataganai* that his son should serve in the U.S. Army, for he
was an American and not a Japanese. Not only that, but it
might very well turn out to be a unique opportunity for the
Nisei to be fully accepted into American society. If so, that
would be a tremendous blessing for the Japanese community.

I remember vividly the community party for the two boys
who were the first Nisei draftees from the White River Val-

ley in the fall of 1939. Issei and Nisei, Christians and Buddhists, were present; and the community, heretofore seldom at one on anything, was solidly united. I shall never forget the message of the village elder, who was not a Christian. It was to the effect that the Issei was wedded to the United States and therefore, though Japan had remained his "original" home for these many years, his "true" home was none other than the United States. The traditional Japanese teaching emphasizes that, once married, the bride must accept her husband's parents as her own, his home as hers; and her primary and ultimate loyalty must be to his parents and his home. "So," said he, "we the Issei gladly offer you, our sons, to the cause of the U.S. Be brave and prove yourselves loyal citizens of this country, for by so doing you will prove worthy inheritors of the best of the Japanese heritage as well."

I rather doubt that this line of thought made a very profound impression on the Nisei, but I have not a shred of doubt that it impressed the Issei tremendously. The metaphor of marriage hit the nail on the head for the Issei much harder than the elder might have expected, for it was very pertinent to his situation. When he saw his son standing proudly in a U.S. Army uniform, he knew that he had been wedded to the United States for all these years, even though there had been many in-laws, as it were, who mistreated him. Characteristically Japanese, he would say, "If I were alone, I might choose to return to Japan, but now I have these children, for whose sake I will stick it out to the bitter end."

Even though the speech might not have inspired the Nisei, that new state of Issei mind was a tremendous relief to the Nisei. Now they—Issei and Nisei—instead of arguing about Japan, together turned their attention to Germany and Italy. The war in Europe thus lessened the Issei-Nisei tension, and momentarily the Japanese community achieved a semblance of internal unity.

At that moment the Issei was in a frame of mind that

would easily have led him to fight the Japanese forces, should they invade the Pacific Coast. Emotionally it would have been an extremely painful thing for him to do, but he would have done it just the same, for he saw quite clearly that it was the only thing for him to do as one who had been "wedded" to the United States. The traditional Japanese ethic, when faithfully adhered to, would not only justify, but more positively demand, his taking the side of the United States.

No Issei, however, articulated his feelings on this extraordinarily touchy subject. Yet, amazingly, this sentiment, in almost everybody's heart, quickly dominated the climate of opinion without anyone's expressing it. There could have been no split within the Japanese-American family insofar as the issue of war between the United States and Japan was concerned, for in that eventuality the Issei would stand solidly behind the Nisei.

3 The Japanese-American Community: A Profile

The Japanese-American community in the late 1930's had become a highly complex society within a society. To many Americans it appeared to be a tightly knit ethnic society whose members were, without exception, aliens whose real home was Japan. In point of fact, however, there was no unity within that community. The common ethnic and national origin and the common predicament in America drove them together in order to maintain a sense of security. What was a racial ghetto from the American point of view had become a haven from the Japanese-American point of view.

In a society in which ethnic minorities are segregated on a group basis, the individuals affected are compelled to find, in the last resort, their security in ethnic solidarity. And that does not in the least justify the frequently heard statement of those favoring segregation: "They prefer to be with their own people, don't they?" It is not that they prefer it; they are simply given no other choice!

Inside the Japanese community, however, were found many divisions and tensions. The principal division was that between Issei and Nisei, both in terms of their relationship to each other and in terms of their respective relationships to Japan and to America.

That division had three notable characteristics. First, there was an enormous gap in the age distribution of the community, so that it was a community of the old and the young, without young adults or those in early middle age. The Issei group became stale as the years went by, while the Nisei section had a long way to go to reach maturity. This meant that the community was bisected in such a way that there was little continuity between the two parts. The community in which there is no group in the thirty-forty age bracket to mediate between the group of fifty years and up and the group of twenty years and under, cannot be a healthy organism. The Nisei and Issei were either opposed to, or turning away from, each other; consequently, there was not much communication of ideas between them.

That, I think, accounts for the almost total lack of knowledge of Japanese culture among the Nisei. The Japan of the Issei was that which he knew when he had left home, and upon which he now looked back through a glass strongly colored by idealization. He would not have found a place for himself in Japan had he returned there in the 1930's. In spite of the loud cry of nationalism and outspoken antiforeignism, Westernization had long been the dynamic of Japan's national economy and social structure. In fact, Western civilization had penetrated into Japan much more thoroughly than into the Japanese community in America.

When, therefore, the Issei emphatically supported the "glorious" war effort of Japan in the 1930's, and when he sent packages to relatives in Japan to help Japanese soldiers in Manchuria, he was like a football fan rooting for his favorite team. His act indicated emotional self-identification

with the team, but not actual participation in the game itself. All this was distasteful to the Nisei, and he would have
tolerated it as an idiosyncrasy of the oldster had it not been
for the danger it might bring upon the Nisei's position in
American society. The Nisei was just as emotional in this as
the Issei, and he could not see anything good in anything
Japan was doing at home or abroad. Neither Issei nor
Nisei, of course, knew much about contemporary Japan,
nor had either of them any real stake in Japan.

Second, from what has been said above, one can see that
the Japanese-American community was divided into two
distinct sections culturally. The Issei was driven, both by his
longing for his homeland and by the social pressure now
spearheaded by the Nisei, into remaining conservative, or
even backward, while the Nisei, deliberately turning his
back upon Japan and overly eager to be known as an American, had become a two hundred per cent American, whose
patriotism was distinguished more by anti-Japanese sentiment and its expression than by anything else.

This cultural division had rather interesting consequences.
In the early period the Issei had thought that it would be a
distinct advantage for his children to know both Japan and
America. By the beginning of the 1930's the Issei had ceased
to think in those terms and had come to accept it as his fate
that he should remain forever a Japanese, while his children
would be Americans.

The Issei, however, continued to insist that the least his
Nisei children ought to do for him was to learn the Japanese
language. Quite simply, what he wanted was that his Nisei
children should be able to talk in Japanese to him in his
old age, since he could never master English. At the same
time, the Issei accepted the Nisei's destiny to be American
remarkably well. He made up his mind to give his children
the best education he could possibly afford, so that they
might excel their fellow Americans. This attitude became

so prevalent among the Japanese that it almost determined the social climate of their community. No parent was satisfied to see his child go no further than high school. The Issei sacrificed much in order to send his sons and daughters to college or at least vocational schools of post-high school standard. College education was so commonplace among the Japanese Americans in the late 1930's that those who did not go to college usually had quite severe reasons for it.

By 1940 there were not yet many college graduates among the Nisei and, therefore, not many educated unemployed. To be sure, there were M.A.'s and Ph.D.'s who, because of their Japanese origin, had been denied employment despite their academic achievement and professional skills, and one used to hear about them from time to time. But the number of them was not yet so great as to affect the climate of opinion among the Nisei.

If the Issei was enough of an old-fashioned Japanese to give the best he could offer to his children, the Nisei was American enough not to give a second thought to his departure from his father's culture. Looking back, one could even say that the attitude of resignation and acceptance on the part of the Issei should have made it totally unnecessary for the Nisei to turn against him so violently. Furthermore, the cultural and psychological distance between the two generations might also have served as a safety valve when the friction between them became serious. The significant thing, however, was the fact that the Issei continued to be so unchangeably Japanese that he remained a wonderfully faithful parent to his Nisei children. This parental love, so much a part of Japanese culture and probably intensified by the sociological factors in America, enabled the Issei to be exceedingly tolerant of much of the Nisei's behavior, which, under ordinary circumstances, would not be either understood or appreciated by any self-respecting Japanese. In the end, the Issei turned out to be as indulgent a parent as his

American counterpart, who badly spoils his children but seldom makes them angry enough to turn against him.

When we look at the religious situation in the community, we find the same picture. In 1939 there were many Japanese Christian congregations in the three states on the Pacific Coast and elsewhere. In spite of the number of organized congregations, the total number of Christians among the Issei was disappointingly small. By and large the Issei had no violent feeling against Christianity as a religion, but most of them felt that inasmuch as they were going to end their life as Japanese, they had better hang on to their ancestral religion. However, since their children were going to be Americans, they might as well adopt the religion of the land and become Christians if they wished. Consequently, in many a family the parents remained Buddhists, while the children were enrolled in Christian Sunday schools and were not infrequently baptized with the parents' consent and approval.

In terms of professed and committed church members, the number of Christians among Nisei was not very large. In terms of the moral concept, outlook on life, and view on human relations, the Nisei generally were more Christian than Buddhist, which was quite natural. They felt more at home at almost any Christian church service than at the Buddhist service. The Buddhist churches were predominantly Issei affairs, to which Nisei activities were merely appended. It was only after the war that Buddhism became a vital religious factor among the Nisei.

Thus, the Japanese-American community was also divided religiously. The division was remarkably clear-cut: Issei—Japanese in culture and nationality, Buddhist in religion; Nisei—American and Christian. The Issei were already past middle age, and the Nisei were barely past adolescence. The former were separated from Japan by the Pacific Ocean and the ever-increasing distance of time, and the latter were segregated from American society by barriers of social discrimination and race prejudice. Such was the pathetic situation of the Japanese-American community in 1939.

4 Reluctant Host

New Year's Day is, for every Japanese, the greatest of all feast days. Its celebration is an act of thanksgiving for safe passage through the year that has just ended. The emphasis is wholly on the old year and all its events, rather than on the coming year, with its sorrows and blessings hidden from human eyes. It is for this reason that one who has lost immediate relatives in the year past refrains not only from celebrating the day but also from extending his greetings to others. In fact, he requests others not to extend their usual greetings to him.

New Year's Day, 1942, was a bleak day for the Japanese community in America. There was neither gaiety nor the usual celebration. Rather, the whole community seemed to be observing a period of formal mourning. Not only had the year just ended been an unfortunate one for it, but the new year was making an ominous entrance. Pearl Harbor and the whole series of events that followed had been a profoundly shocking experience, and the immediate future looked even more disturbing.

Atmosphere of Fear

The attack on Pearl Harbor had been followed immediately by the nightmare of FBI round-ups, which deeply upset the community. Had their hearts been more with Japan than with the United States, they would have taken the FBI activity as quite justifiable and would have endured it without complaint. Because they had so completely identified themselves, in their own minds at least, with America, they interpreted that action as hostile and as a betrayal of their loyalty.

Beginning with the morning of December 8, I commuted daily between Kent and Seattle, visiting the families of those interned by the FBI and other individuals upset and fearful about what was going to happen next. I also consulted with the leaders of the Seattle Council of Churches on many matters that pertained to the well-being of the Japanese people. I even paid a visit to the FBI office, simply to let them know that I was available as an interpreter in cases where they might encounter language difficulty. Subsequently I did assist in that capacity on several occasions.

In no time, however, the whole community was thoroughly panic-stricken; every male lived in anticipation of arrest by the FBI, and every household endured each day in fear and trembling. Most Japanese, including at least one clergyman, were so afraid of being marked by association with those who had been taken away that they hesitated to visit the wives and children of the victims. Much of that fear can be attributed to the rumors, rampant in the community, about the grounds for those arrests, about the treatment the detainees were getting, and about their probable imprisonment for the duration of the war. No rational explanation could set their minds at ease.

As for myself, I can say one thing: despite all that was happening, I retained my faith in American fairness and justice. Deep in my heart, I was positive that Americans were not out to torment the Japanese. I knew many Americans too well to believe that as a group they intended to be cruel or to hurt us. But war is war, and since Japan was the enemy, we could not expect to be treated as if we were not Japanese.

Quite as important as my faith in America, however, was my unshakeable faith in the Japanese people in America. By virtue of my intimate knowledge of the Japanese community, I knew full well that, in spite of an occasional outburst of boisterous pro-Japanese sentiment, there was not a Japanese in America who would do anything to harm the United States. They were too fond of their children and were too dependent on them to jeopardize their position as American citizens. I thus had an invincible confidence in the innocence of the Japanese. That confidence, coupled with my belief in the basic fairness of the American people, made it unbelievably easy for me to carry on my self-appointed ministry of reconciliation in those days.

There were pathetic incidents, however. Almost everybody burned books and magazines in the Japanese language, because rumor had it that the FBI agents had found Japanese books in the possession of those who had been picked up. The books burned were not generally of any great value, I am certain, but occasionally there were items of enormous worth. For example, one Mr. Kobayashi, an intellectual peddler, announced to me that he had burned up the whole series of the works of Uchimura Kanzo. He said to me, "I had been hoping that you would show up. I did not dare call you up by telephone. I wanted you to take my Uchimura *Zenshu* ["Collected Works"]. But I finally had to burn them, lest the FBI got here before you did." Uchimura was a Christian prophet in modern Japan and a prolific writer. He had studied at Amherst College in Massachusetts in the 1880's, and knew America exceedingly well. He had been highly critical of the Oriental Exclusion Act, and that above everything else had frightened Mr. Kobayashi.

In addition to book burning there were other ugly things

happening. For example, the insurance companies were canceling as bad risks the insurance policies covering automobiles owned by Japanese. This sort of thing made one wonder whether hysteria might not have given place to reason. One heard about little incidents here and there of Americans being nasty to Japanese for no reason other than to show their misguided patriotism. All these incidents were all too human, and perhaps one should not have been alarmed. But they had a cumulative effect that was damaging, and not to be deeply affected by these incidents was not easy. It was during that trying period that an unexpected incident happened to me.

On December 30, I spent the day in Seattle calling on families. When my friend and colleague, the Rev. N. Kodaira of the Presbyterian Church, a bachelor clergyman like me, fell ill, I drove him to the Columbus Hospital and stayed until he was settled. Then I started back for Kent. I was just about home when, without any warning, a car smashed head-on into my car. My car was a total wreck, but miraculously I got out without a scratch. When I walked over to the other car, I found the driver dead drunk, muttering to himself, "Did I hit somebody?" I was at my wit's end to know what to do. But seeing that he was not very seriously injured, though bleeding rather badly from his face, I decided to walk the quarter-mile to my home and call the sheriff's office. At that moment a car stopped, and out came an Army officer. He asked me first whether I was a Japanese, and then proceeded to question me about my being on the highway late at night. He inspected the contents of my brief case, the book of minutes, in Japanese, of the Seattle Federation of Japanese Churches, of which I was then secretary. He then drove me home and announced that he would call the sheriff's office and report the accident.

I should have stayed at home, but I was extremely anxious about the other fellow. Besides, I did not want to be away from the scene of the accident when the sheriff got there. So

I phoned the sheriff's office myself, reported the accident, and walked back to the spot. In a couple of minutes the sheriff arrived, and I was busy giving him the details when the Army officer returned. Finding me talking with the sheriff, he immediately announced that I was under arrest, ordered one of his subordinates to search me, and then asked the sheriff whether he had any objection to turning me over to the U.S. Army. The sheriff answered, "I have nothing to say to the U.S. Army."

I was then taken to the King County jail. On the way, I turned to the Army officer and said, "You know, I left my bedroom light burning."

He answered, "I doubt very much that the planes of your country will come this far tonight." Then he added, "Your country is at war with us. You should not be out at night like this. I'm sorry I have to do this to you, but I have no other choice."

And so I was a guest of the county. I must admit that I was not very sleepy. When morning came, before I could phone my bishop to tell him where I was, the same Army officer returned and said, "Father, I apologize for the rough treatment of last night. We went back to Kent and inquired about you. You have an excellent reputation. We have nothing against you whatsoever." On release, I walked over to the bishop's and found that he had already been notified of my arrest and was at that moment on his way to bail me out.

I relate that episode because it made an indelible impression on me. The scene of that accident became the Bethel (Gen. 28:10-22) in the pilgrimage of my life. Every time I have been faced with a rough situation, I have said to myself, "Suppose I had been killed at that time." I began to live as though on borrowed time and did not spare myself in serving those committed to my charge. The incident also confirmed my trust in the basic fairness of Americans. Many of my American friends were furious about what had happened. Personally, I did not feel that I had been unjustly treated, though I was equally convinced that what the officer did was totally unnecessary.

A Rumor About Evacuation Spreads

Shortly after the New Year started, a rumor began to spread to the effect that all Japanese in America would be rounded up and moved to some remote place. Where that rumor originated, it was extremely difficult to know. Probably we shall never know whether it was deliberately planted by some person or group with a definite objective in mind or whether it had somehow been born out of the peculiar social climate then prevailing; at any rate, once started, it gained momentum from one day to the next.

Rational reaction to that rumor would have been to say that, if such a measure was necessary at all, it was in the period immediately following the attack on Pearl Harbor, but the time had now passed, and the United States was completely mobilized. There was no real possibility that the forces of Japan would invade the West Coast.

I could not believe that such mass evacuation was seriously being considered by any sane person. I failed to see any necessity, military or otherwise, for such a measure. On the contrary, I could see the folly of it. Frankly, I thought that neither the American government nor the American public would be so stupid as to allow such a thing to happen. But I soon discovered that I was not quite right. It was announced that a specially appointed congressional committee, headed by Rep. John H. Tolan of California, was to conduct a series of public hearings in the major West Coast cities to determine whether such a measure was necessary. Only then did it become clear that some people believed that those of Japanese descent on the Pacific Coast were dangerous to the national security and advised—in what manner I do not know—the national government to remove them from the coastal area. And it was also quite clear that

great pressure was being put on the federal government by
a number of West Coast groups.*

Spearheading a large number of organizations were the
Joint Committee on Oriental Immigration and the Native
Sons and Daughters of the Golden West, both organizations
of superpatriots. Carey McWilliams' exposé of all those
groups leaves no question in his readers' minds that most of
them had economic interests which made them eager to
eliminate the Japanese from the arena of business competition, despite their organizational claims to be defenders of
free enterprise and to be utterly opposed to any kind of
social planning or business control. To brand a people as
ineligible to enter the arena of business competition on
grounds of race, religion, or national origin is always an easy
way to reduce competition while upholding the competitive
system. The use of this device has long helped racial prejudice to perpetuate itself in American society.

These "patriotic" groups seized the crisis created by the
Japanese attack on Pearl Harbor to make a well-organized
and concerted effort to eliminate, once and for all, people of
Japanese descent from West Coast states.

Besides pressuring the federal government through their
representatives in Congress, these "patriotic" groups agitated
the public by all sorts of propaganda and loose talk. What
was some of this loose talk? Let me list samples at random. It
was said that in the event of invasion of the Pacific Coast by
Japanese forces, the Japanese and their Nisei children would
more than likely take sides with Japan, and therefore their
continued residence in the coastal area was a menace to the
national security. This was a highly conjectural speculation
which did not fail to arouse interest. Some people deliberately planted this notion and saw it spread like wildfire. In
the course of its travel from mouth to mouth, from one re-

---

*See Carey McWilliams' *Brothers Under the Skin* and *Prejudice; Japanese
Americans: Symbol of Racial Intolerance* for information about these
groups and their motives.

gion to another, it picked up momentum, with new ideas tacked on to it, and the original idea became more and more exaggerated. In the end it became a tremendously powerful determinant of public opinion.

It was also said that the Japanese stayed on the West Coast just for this kind of situation. From the beginning they had had this in mind, and had been planning it all these years. To prove such a thesis, it was remarked: "Look at where they live, or where they farm. They are always near strategic industries." In the Seattle area, for instance, there were a number of farmers very near the Boeing airplane assembly plant. But the fact was that they had been there for years before the Boeing factory was established. Strawberry farmers on the Bainbridge Islands and oyster planters in Olympia Bay were credited with having chosen these strategic spots in relation to the Bremerton Navy Yard. Had it been objectionable from the military point of view, they would never have been allowed to live and work in those areas. Furthermore, in every case the Japanese did not own the farms. They usually leased from, or at best were partners with, white people.

It was also said that the Japanese were sneaky, as was proved by the way they attacked Pearl Harbor. They could be reasonable for years and years, but then something would snap and make them mean and treacherous. They could never be fully trusted. This notion inevitably led to the next: all Japanese are potential saboteurs. For example, many Japanese who worked for the railroads were discharged, for fear they might commit acts of sabotage.

Such were the arguments being offered for a policy of mass evacuation. The horrible part of it was that loose talk continuously filled the air, conditioning the attitude of people toward anybody who even looked Japanese. People of Chinese and Filipino origin suffered from mistaken identification, and they began to wear badges saying "I am a Chinese [or Filipino] American." When two or three Japanese exchanged greetings at a street corner in Japanese, they were immediately suspected of plotting something dangerous. White Americans who continued to be friendly with Japanese were also liable to suspicion. Like an infected body, American society on the Pacific Coast was rapidly disintegrating from within.

Yet despite that hysteria, the personal relationships long established between the Japanese people and their neighbors or business associates suffered little in some places. I know for a fact that there were many white Americans who took an enormous amount of trouble to make known to the county sheriff, municipal authorities, and other public officials their willingness to vouch for their Japanese neighbors and to be responsible for them. These friends of Japanese families invariably said that they could not generalize on all Japanese, but they knew this or that family, had lived next to them for years, their kids had gone to school with the kids of the Japanese family; and knowing the particular family, they therefore felt there was no reason to be afraid of allowing them to live where they were. The reassuring words and conduct of such friends kept the Japanese from complete discouragement when the general trend of public opinion was going from bad to worse, week by week.

The Tolan Committee Hearings

In the middle of that public hysteria, the House Committee on National Defense Migration, with Rep. John H. Tolan as chairman, began to conduct its series of West Coast hearings on the need for the mass evacuation of the Japanese. I attended the public session held in Seattle. The one regret that I have about my activities in connection with the wartime plight of the Japanese people is that I did not testify at that hearing. True, no one had asked me to. True, also, I was then in the United States on a temporary visitor's visa and therefore had neither right nor obligation to take part. True, likewise, that I felt whatever I might say would not be listened to because I was a Japanese, and whatever I might say could be said just as well, if not better, by a number of Americans in whom I had the profoundest trust. So I rationalized to my own satisfaction. But today I cannot help feeling that I should have publicly registered what I felt. I am sure that it would have made no difference whatsoever as far as the government's policy was concerned, but at least a wider circle of thoughtful citizens might have learned what some thoughtful Japanese were then thinking. I did not do what I felt I should do because I was not sure of myself and, therefore, afraid. Afraid of what? I knew not then, and I know not now, exactly what it was that I had to fear, for I did write and publish "An Open Letter to American Christians" (in *The Living Church* and *The St. Andrews Cross*), going on record with exactly what I thought about the proposed mass evacuation. The closest I can now come to identifying that fear was that I would make a fool of myself. Yes, I was a coward, for I did not dare express what I was convinced was the truth because of all sorts of secondary considerations. Regardless of the consequences, I should have stood before the Tolan Committee and testified.

As for the hearing, only one thing stands out vividly in my memory—the testimony of Floyd Schmoe, Professor of Forestry at the University of Washington, then on leave to direct the work of the American Friends Service Committee. The period of his testimony was unusually long—much longer than most of the others—but the greater part of the time was spent in cross-examining his position on pacifism, a belief which he held as a Quaker. Insofar as my memory goes, it was not the Japanese people, but Floyd Schmoe himself, whose loyalty was being questioned. I thought it was utterly unfair to Floyd, and even to this day I marvel at the patience with which he sat through that excruciating cross-examination. I am certain he bore it only because he felt the destiny of the Japanese Americans was at stake. I am glad that I heard his testimony, for in the subsequent months and years there were many moments when I was sorely

tempted to become skeptical and cynical about the motives
and purposes of the many well-meaning Americans.

The Community Becomes Morbid

The whole Japanese community reacted to the general situation as one man. There was no one conspicuously leading
the community, for all the elders had been interned by the
FBI. Those left in the community were sorely afraid. Church
services were just about the only gatherings that went
on uninterrupted. And yet the Japanese community felt,
thought, and reacted like a solid, well-organized group. It was
indeed uncanny.

Both as individuals and as a community the Japanese
found it utterly impossible to cope with the attack upon
them. To counter the loose talk and rumor, what could they
have done? The only thing they could do to defend themselves was to talk about themselves—how loyal they were to
the United States. But the more they talked about themselves
and their loyalty to the United States, the less they were believed. Thus they were driven into a situation where their
only choice was either to keep silent and suffer all sorts of
slander or to defend themselves against those slanders by
talking.

This was quite a contrast to the situation in Hawaii, where
there was no time for people to indulge in talk. When bombs
were dropping, everybody risked his life to defend his country. The Japanese in Hawaii did not need to proclaim how
loyal they were; they proved it by their actions. Accordingly,
they were not targets of idle talk based on speculation.

The Japanese community soon entered a morbid state of
internal friction. After the initial round-up of community
leaders, the FBI continued to investigate individuals, and
here and there a few more men were taken into custody almost every day. Seeing the Japanese American Citizens
League (JACL) making every conceivable effort to impress
the American public with the patriotism of the Nisei, some

of the Issei began to suspect that the Nisei might have been acting as informants for the FBI. To my knowledge there was nothing of the sort done by any Nisei, but their compulsive desire to prove their loyalty in the face of the mounting antipathy against them gave the impression that they would do anything to prove themselves.

The JACL in 1940 was primarily an educational organization that emphasized keeping the Nisei community informed about the civic and political scene. At any rate, young and frail though it was, the JACL was the only Nisei organization anything like a representative body of Japanese Americans. Up to that time it had been a really small group, for there had not been very many Nisei old enough to be interested in it.

The JACL leadership was afraid of having too close a relationship with the Issei, but without Issei contributions it could not possibly carry on its activities. Objectively speaking, there was no denying that the JACL was in the long run doing tremendous good for the Issei as well as for the Nisei. To the Issei, however, it did not appear that way. They felt that their money was used by the Nisei exclusively for the Nisei, and sometimes to the disadvantage of the Issei. When hundreds of Issei were being detained by the FBI, the JACL did not do anything to get them released. The fact of the matter was that no one knew where to begin.

The Plight of the Farmers

Those were really bad days for the Japanese in America. To speak from my own experiences in the White River Valley, the plight of Japanese farmers was beyond imagination. While the air was filled with rumors that they would be removed, the farmers had to plan for their growing season. In that area January and February are the time to prepare the soil for planting. If they were to be removed, then what? No simple answer could be given. In dealing with that question, I had a firsthand experience of the inherent difficulty with democracy, and more specifically with the interdepartmental inconsistencies within a democratic government. While the Tolan Committee was moving from Seattle to Los Angeles, conducting public hearings, men of good will talked to various government agencies in an attempt to sound out what the position of the federal government was likely to be, and to influence the government to take constructive action.

From these men we heard that the Department of Justice was decidedly against a mass evacuation and was confident that the FBI had the situation well under control. In the state of Washington every county sheriff was reported to be absolutely sure that he could cope with the situation. On top of these reassuring reports, we heard that the Department of Agriculture was extremely eager for the Japanese farmers to double their agricultural production of foodstuffs. The worst that could happen, it seemed, would be selective evacuation. The farmers, then, should be the last ones to be removed, unless their farms were located near strategic war industries or military establishments.

Thus reassured, the Japanese farmers made up their minds to go ahead with their work; but when they went to the bank or to the dealers, they were denied credit, on the grounds that they might not be there for more than a few weeks. They could purchase fertilizer and seeds for cash, but not on credit. Nine out of ten Japanese farmers did not have enough cash on hand. The only recourse left for them was to sit tight and wait. They soon discovered that they could not even sit tight and wait in peace, for people began to talk about their "sabotaging" while the nation was experiencing an acute shortage of vegetables and other foodstuffs.

Daily I was asked by the Japanese farmers just what they should do. I could not even advise them to sit tight any more. One day, with young Bill Taketa, the chairman of the White River Valley chapter of the JACL, I called on the mayor of Kent, Maj. Richard Gooden, a veteran of the First World War. I put it up to Mayor Gooden that the plight of the

Japanese farmers deserved his serious attention and that something should be done about it. I presented my problem of what to tell the Japanese people in the face of contradictory statements. He agreed to let the JACL chapter call a general meeting of all the Japanese in the area, to which spokesmen for various government agencies would be invited to speak.

When the meeting was held, the mayor himself was present with the chief of police and the chairman of the civilian defense committee. With young Taketa presiding and myself as interpreter, men from several government agencies explained what the Japanese farmers were expected to do. What did that meeting accomplish? Nothing, insofar as anything tangible was concerned. Obviously, no one was able to tell exactly what was going to happen. All they could say was that they sympathized with the farmers and would do everything in their power to ease the difficulty; in the meantime, the Japanese should keep their chins up and do their best. Futile and meaningless, you say? Some might have thought so. I felt, and even to this day I have continued to feel, that that meeting was one of the most memorable incidents of those days. It was no small thing for several hundred Japanese to have a meeting without inviting any protest or criticism from the local people. It was no small thing for the Japanese farmers to be addressed by official representatives of the national government.

The Evacuation Order Issued

On March 2, 1942—the day on which the Tolan Committee was to report back to Washington—Lt. Gen. John L. DeWitt, commanding general of the Western Defense Command, issued his infamous evacuation order. His issuance of that order before the Committee even made their report clearly gave the impression that the public hearings were a farce to pretend that the forthcoming evacuation order was based on the will of the public. Obviously, much more preparation than the series of public hearings must have been made, for almost simultaneously with the evacuation order there was also announced the creation of the Wartime Civil Control Administration (WCCA) to supervise the evacuation. Within a few weeks the President created, by executive order, a civilian agency, the War Relocation Authority (WRA), to look after the problems which would arise as a result of evacuation.

The evacuation order issued by Lt. Gen. DeWitt designated the western half of the states of Washington and Oregon, the entire state of California, and a portion of Arizona a military defense zone from which anybody of Japanese blood, even one-sixteenth Japanese blood, had to remove himself. The order allowed the Japanese people to move out of the area voluntarily, but after a given date all movement by Japanese from the area was to be "frozen." "Voluntary" evacuation as quickly as possible was encouraged. A few Seattle families with friends in areas outside of the military zone ventured to pack up their belongings and moved eastward. Although there were some colonies of Japanese in eastern Washington, eastern Oregon, Idaho, Nebraska, and Colorado, the communities in those areas were not in the mood to welcome a large number of Japanese from the West Coast, for fear that they, too, might become targets of suspicion and criticism. Far more serious was the attitude of the American public toward the Japanese evacuees as they traveled. It was not long before the newspapers reported that the governors of all the western states, with the exception of Colorado, refused to give the WRA assurance of their cooperation for the safety of Japanese who might relocate in their respective states.

The WCCA officers in charge of processing the "voluntary" evacuation made it clear that once families left the military zone, they would not be allowed to re-enter. That was a harsh order. The Japanese people were to leave their

homes, but their safety—the most elementary right of a human being in a civilized society—seemed to be denied to
them. How could they take such a step? Only a handful
blessed by a combination of favorable conditions ventured
to move eastward. The great majority had to stay where they
were. When thousands of Japanese refugees failed to trek
across the Cascade Mountains, they were criticized for sabotaging the government's effort.

The Preliminaries to Evacuation

Spring in the White River Valley is exceedingly beautiful.
I vividly recall the smiling faces of boys and girls helping
their parents in their gardens. I used to make all my pastoral
calls right in the fields. Easter Sunday I would wonder who
were those pretty, well-dressed young ladies kneeling at the
communion rail, for seldom had I seen them in anything
other than blue jeans. From the middle of February on,
wherever I went, I used to see men driving tractors and cul-
tivating the land, the girls and women busy handling seed-
lings in the hothouse. The spring air, filled with the fra-
grance of all kinds of flowers, was vibrant with life.

The spring of 1942 was entirely different. When I drove
around the Valley, few people greeted me. The whole valley
looked deserted. When I knocked at the kitchen door—only
strangers who had to be formal went to the front door—I
was greeted by voices filled with anxiety and fear.

Toward the end of March we began to hear about one
place in California after another having been given two
weeks' notice to get ready for mass evacuation. Even then we
did not quite believe that we, too, might be in the same
boat. We just could not imagine how such a thing could
come upon that beautiful and peaceful valley, where people
had remained remarkably friendly all those weeks.

Around the first of April, we saw orders posted all over
the Valley on telephone poles, announcing the last day of the

period of "voluntary" evacuation, after which we would
have to remain "frozen." Curfew laws were also to be en-
forced—we would have to stay at home from 8 P.M. to 6 A.M.
A few families finally made up their minds and left for eastern Oregon or Idaho just before the deadline. I cannot forget the sadness that filled me when on my familiar rounds I
came upon a house just vacated, and did not find the smiling
faces of the children who used to greet me. I somehow had
to get out of my car and, like a man possessed, walk around
the house. When, I asked myself, would I see my parishion-
ers again—if at all?

How long could we stay? That was the next question.
Could we remain until after the first harvest? Otherwise,
why couldn't they remove us tomorrow? It was really deadly
for the farmers to have to stay on their farms without doing
anything. Every one of them would have been extremely
happy to double his efforts to produce, had they been assured
that they would be allowed to stay until after the harvest.

In late April, I was given a special permit to ride with
Deaconess Peppers out to the Puyallup Assembly Center to
pay my last pastoral call on the congregation of St. Peter's
Mission, Seattle. They were herded into the fair grounds,
confined behind barbed wire, and guarded by armed sen-
tries. It was all too brief a visit, but no visit was ever more
profoundly appreciated. I shall never forget how struck I was
by the smiles on people's faces when they saw me coming
through the gate. Children flocked to greet me. And those
people, who little short of two weeks before had been under
such tension and anxiety, were now completely relaxed, even
though they had lost, however temporarily it might prove
to be, all the comforts of human habitation. To be sure, the
eyes of the women who saw me off were filled with tears, but
we somehow knew that it was not the last time we would
see one another. I knew that once they reached their destination, it would not be too bad for them. No comfort or

pleasure would be awaiting them, to be sure; but certainly no concentration camp like those in Nazi Germany.

The Silence of the Churches

The churches had been curiously silent for all those months, except that at almost every hearing of the Tolan Committee there were church representatives testifying against any mass evacuation. But there had been no organized effort made by the Christian churches to prevent such a measure's being adopted by the government. It was obvious that churchmen were opposed to it as a matter of principle, but nothing was done beyond that.* Undesirable though it was, once the evacuation order was issued, the church leaders began to say that under the circumstances it probably was the wisest thing for the government to do; it was for the safety of the loyal and innocent Japanese people. We were to be put under protective custody, lest we be attacked or molested under the pressure of wartime hysteria.

The evacuation order was unquestionably a defeat for the forces of justice. All the Christian virtues—humility, long-suffering, forgiveness, self-sacrifice, magnanimity and tolerance—were to be practiced by the victims (most of whom were not even Christians), while the oppressors, the majority of whom were at least nominally Christians, were not to be blamed for their organized robbery. I am not saying this in the spirit of criticism against the American churches, for I was a partner in that guilt. I record it as the self-criticism in depth of the Christian Church itself. For not to acknowledge that defeat before the organized forces of injustice is to add another sin—the sin of hypocrisy—to the record.

* As to the action taken by the Christian churches following the outbreak of war on December 7, 1941, reference should be made to Toru Matsumoto's *Beyond Prejudice* (Friendship Press, 1946). Matsumoto modestly says that his is *a* story and not the *whole* story, which of course is true. Nevertheless, one can get a good picture of what the Protestant churches did in the years following Pearl Harbor, until the end of 1945.

The Injustice of the Evacuation Order

On the other hand, the U.S. government has made it extremely difficult for the Japanese in America to blame it for any misfortune, hardship, or economic loss they suffered in connection with the evacuation. But the fact remains that the people of Japanese descent were taken into custody without benefit of due process or without having a specific charge lodged against them. Why?

First, the designation of certain geographical areas as military zones was done by the commanding general of the Western Defense Command, on the basis of military necessity and national security. Once the zones were established, there could be no argument as to whom the military regarded unacceptable or why. Lt. Gen. DeWitt's immortal statement, "Once a Jap, always a Jap," was sufficient to remove American citizens of Japanese descent and their alien parents, or to put an alien Japanese and an American citizen of one-sixteenth Japanese blood together in custody, without discrimination. It was made to appear simply a military action, for which the civil government could not be blamed.

Second, the WCCA simply supervised the evacuation, and nothing more. What happened to any family after evacuation was not its concern. To be sure, it provided all sorts of services to help facilitate the evacuation process; but for more pressing problems, such as how to dispose of one's belongings, one's business, or one's debts, the WCCA had nothing concrete to offer. The final decision had to be made by each evacuee. The government did not confiscate anything that belonged to the evacuee; neither had it anything to do with his business transactions. Whether the evacuee made a profit or lost money was his responsibility, not the government's.

The extraordinary thing that marked those days was that the distinction between the Issei and the Nisei was temporarily reduced to nil. To maintain at least a semblance of democracy, the Nisei, as citizens, should have been permitted to make their own choice: to go with their parents or to stay. Had that been allowed, it would of course have defeated the intent of those groups which wanted to eliminate the Japanese from the arena of business competition once and for all. The order therefore treated the Nisei and their children (Sansei) exactly the same as the Issei. Young men of draft age were all reclassified as "enemy aliens," thus exempting them from military duty. At long last a sign of consistency was seen, for the Nisei were strongly advised that they had no other way to show their patriotism than by cooperating with the WCCA and being evacuated quietly. From the standpoint of the Japanese community, it would have been a practical impossibility to separate the Nisei from the Issei then, for the majority of the Nisei were not yet ready to take over the businesses of their parents.

5 Unwilling Journey

On Mother's Day weekend (May 10-12), 1942, we who were living in the White River Valley and its surrounding areas found ourselves on the evacuation trains, destination unknown. I had been busy until the very last minute handling countless details—legal, financial, domestic, personal—for my helpless companions. For example, it had taken endless negotiations with a number of agencies to secure permission for one tubercular patient to stay in the sanatorium. On the day before the first train was to leave, I had happened to meet at the hospital a young Nisei woman, married to a Filipino, who had just had a baby. Neither she nor her husband knew for sure whether she and their children were entitled to stay where they were or, if they had to be evacuated, whether her husband was entitled to accompany them to camp. The evacuation order was quite clear on that point: anyone of Japanese blood, of whatever degree, must be evacuated. Whether this resulted in a temporary separation of that man from his wife and children or whether he accompanied his family to the camp, I no longer remember. Most likely the young mother and her children caught one of the

three trains while her husband remained behind, hoping
that in the not-too-distant future arrangements could be
made for their reunion.

Preliminaries of Departure

Prior to departure every family and every individual had
to be registered. When registration was completed, each family or individual was given a family number.

The official instructions advised each person to take with
him only as much as he could carry. The rest of his belongings were to be sold or left behind. The WCCA provided a
warehouse where anything we wanted to keep could be
stored for the duration, free of charge. Most of our families
were rather poor farmers, few owned furniture really worth
storing, and most of them had debts which they managed to
pay off by selling the greater part of their belongings. We
had also converted our mission building into a storehouse
where families might bring their things. As for myself, I did
not own anything except books that needed special care. I
put my library together and sent it to my good friend Lewis
Bailey, the rector of Trinity Parish, Seattle. What few
clothes and things of that sort I owned, were neatly put in a
small trunk, which I left with Deaconess Peppers. My own
problem was thus extremely simple. But a family who had
lived in one place for ten, twenty, or thirty years, with five
or six or, in some cases, even seven or eight children, heavily
in debt and without resources, had only one choice: to sell
everything they could not take with them.

Consequently, there were hundreds of private auctions
going on simultaneously all over the Valley, at which pov-
erty-stricken Japanese farmers were parting with most of
their worldly possessions as their creditors and other greed-
ridden buyers purchased them for practically nothing. Those
not in debt hastily liquidated large items like pianos, refrig-
erators, davenports, automobiles, and tractors. Some were
fortunate enough, to be sure, to have long-standing and

trustworthy neighbors or friends among Caucasian Americans—how regrettable that that phrase need be used—who would look after such things for them; and in some instances, these friends became caretakers of homes and farms—lock, stock, and barrel. Such cases, however, were not numerous. In addition, many could not bring themselves to trust the government and generally did not take advantage of the provisions for free storage because they feared that after they had been evacuated, somebody would set fire to the buildings in which their precious possessions were stored. How could anybody assure them that no such thing would happen, after what had already occurred despite all the assurances and reassurances given by people in whom they had placed their full confidence? "Convert everything saleable into cash while it can be done!" became the motto of many.

What this action meant in legal and economic terms, no one had even begun to comprehend. Few gave a thought to the fact that sooner or later the war would be over and a normal state of affairs would be restored. Everybody was preoccupied with the urgent problems that lay immediately ahead of them: what to do with what had been accumulated over the years, with all those precious things they were not to be allowed to take with them. Everybody worried about what their lives would be in the concentration camps. The aged men, especially, jumped to the conclusion that their sweat and toil of many years was now coming to naught and that they were finished, absolutely finished. There would be no future for them in America. Whatever might happen in the years to follow, they were sure they would not have a chance to reclaim what they were then about to lose.

Being thoroughly Oriental, the Japanese made no noise and showed no visible signs of distress, even though many were frantic. They lost all their business sense and reasoning capacity, and, of course, they were amply taken advantage of. Some were relieved when they had sold off the last item in their houses. Not a few, for the first time in years, had cash in their pockets instead of a batch of loan notes.

Blind Journey

On May 12, which was Mother's Day, Fred Meadowcroft drove me to Renton in the old station wagon in which I used to collect and deliver children before and after Sunday school. Then I turned the car over to him, so that he might dispose of it for the diocese. I had two fair-sized suitcases and a bedroll.

At the Renton railway station, quite a crowd of people gathered to bid us farewell. That to me was a reassuring scene, and made an indelible impression on me. These people had been neighbors and business associates of our families, or schoolmates of our children. They were there as friends whose friendship could not be destroyed. Surrounding us were the fields and hills of the White River Valley, so fresh in their green under the warm sun of mid-May. Presently the train started to move silently. Once more good-byes were exchanged, and the distance between those standing by the tracks and those on the train increased by the second. For quite a number of people on that train, this was the last time they would ever see the Valley.

When it came time for us to depart, we were divided into three groups, the first of which left on May 10. Without hesitation I decided to go with the last group, because I wanted to be available in case of emergency or mishap. I had no fear about the camp to which we were going, having seen what an assembly center was like at Puyallup, though we did not have the faintest idea where it might be.

A number of soldiers, who functioned more or less as conductors, accompanied us. They were all young fellows, most of them friendly and easy to talk to. Soon we were told that all window shades had to be pulled and kept down all the time, without any reason being given. I walked from one end of the long train to the other, just to see how everybody was getting along. When I finally sat down and relaxed for the first time in many days, I immediately fell asleep. But soon I was awakened by children singing; and, lo and behold, the people around me were busy enjoying their lunch. Everybody was settled in his seat, relaxed and looking as if he hadn't a thing in the world to worry about. No one seemed to care where we were being taken. No matter what might be ahead of us, we were all together; and that was the most reassuring thing for the moment. Thus, quite unexpectedly, we had a rather enjoyable journey for, I believe, two days and two nights. It brought us to Pinedale, a few miles outside Fresno, California, which turned out to be our destination.

What time of the day it was when we arrived, I do not remember. From the railroad station we were driven in Army trucks to a place with rows and rows of barracks inside barbed-wire fences. There was inspection of baggage once again, presumably to make sure that no one carried into the camp any contraband articles: short-wave radio sets, firearms, or firewater. Then each family was given one room, into which as many Army cots were brought as there were numbers in the family. There was no other furniture whatever. Single men were steered into bachelors' barracks, a fate which I escaped because I was a clergyman. No one raised any fuss about my receiving such special treatment, and it was not long before I began to have a constant stream of people visiting me with all sorts of complaints and entreating me to present their cases to the camp administration.

Pinedale Assembly Center

The camp, called Pinedale Assembly Center, was run by the WCCA. We were told not to use the term "camp" in referring to it, for it was an assembly center, not a concentration camp. Those in charge of the center were by and large decent and kindly people. Hauk, the head of the center, was a big, tall fellow who sounded tough and officious but was a soft-hearted and even sentimental person inside. Johns, the chief of the internal police, was a fair-minded and masculine sort of fellow. King, another official I still remember, was in charge of community affairs. He was a downright nice fellow, and would do anything to make our life there tolerable. The place was constantly patrolled by military police to prevent any communication with the outside.

In the afternoon of our first day, I tried to take a nap, but had to abandon the attempt—the temperature inside the barracks was 115° F. We who were accustomed to the mild temperatures of the Pacific Northwest were not fit to do anything, even to take a nap, in such heat. The saving grace was that at sundown the temperature dropped suddenly; then the place actually became cool. The price of this comfort was a tremendous sandstorm. And sandstorm it really was, for on the ground there was not a tree, nor even a blade of grass. Just outside the barbed-wire fence were acres and acres of orchards, with fig trees predominating. How I wished I could have sat under the shade of those fig trees! Old Japanese told me that around the turn of the century many, many Japanese who worked in this very valley had died from the heat. Less than ten miles away was the city of Fresno, with a sizable Japanese population. They were being kept, we were told, in the Fresno Fair Grounds.

About a week after we arrived, we were joined by the Japanese community of Tacoma, Washington. They had been our closest neighbors, and we were quite happy to see them. In another week or so, people from the rural counties of Oregon were sent in. This caused no undue excitement. But when a sizable group of Japanese from Sacramento County, California, arrived, the atmosphere of the camp became rather tense, for antagonism arose between the Californians and the Northwesterners, though all were of Japanese descent. It was exceedingly interesting to watch, but there was no time for such a luxury as academic analysis of the situation. What was needed then was some sort of community development program.

First, however, I must tell how the tension came to a head. Looking back on it, all the contributing incidents were really silly, but at Pinedale everything assumed life-and-death importance. For example, knowing how much the Japanese made of their family relationship, the WCCA assured the evacuee Japanese that no family would be separated. This was most reassuring. But many complained that upon arriving at Pinedale, their families had been split up. To be sure, the whole family was at Pinedale—but not in the same barracks. It soon became clear that the WCCA conceived of a family in terms of the nuclear family, while the Japanese thought in terms of the extended family. They wanted to have all the relatives and in-laws clustered together in one building or in immediately neighboring barracks. In the few instances where this request was fulfilled, the beneficiaries soon regretted it, for living so close turned out to be rather trying for the relatives and in-laws.

Even so, many felt that their families had to stick together, and insisted that their housing arrangements be changed. It was no simple matter to rearrange housing for thousands of people, so the administration was extremely reluctant to do anything about these complaints. But where there were good reasons, such as aged couples needing constant care by their married sons or daughters, or chronic invalids needing special care, rearrangements were made. These changes, of course, were made on the basis of the time when one arrived. The Californians, being the latecomers, felt cheated by both Washingtonians and Oregonians.

The Californians and the Northwesterners were, in fact, quite different from each other in many ways. In Oregon and Washington, the Japanese population was far less concentrated than in California. In Sacramento County, I was told, there were public schools attended almost exclusively by children of Japanese parentage. Consequently, the Nisei

from that county spoke Japanese much more fluently than
the Nisei from the Northwest, and their outlook was much
closer to that of the Issei. But love seemed to ignore such
differences. Boys from the Northwest began to show interest
in girls from California, and vice versa. (In fact, there were
romances developing between soldiers on sentry duty and
Nisei girls behind the fence.) All these developments tended
to aggravate an extremely tense situation.

One of the first things I did was to organize church services for the various religious groups. The administration set
aside one barracks as a community hall which was used every
Sunday by the Issei Christians from 9 to 10 A.M., by the Nisei
Christians from 10:30 to 11:30 A.M., and by the Buddhist
group in the afternoon. During the week this community
hall was used for all sorts of purposes by volunteer groups.
For church services clergymen of several denominations co-
operated. On recreational programs volunteers from California and the Northwest, from Christian and Buddhist groups,
worked together. All functions, religious and secular alike,
were open to everybody. There was soon a community newspaper, under the fitting title of *Pinedale Saw Dust,* coming
out every week.

While at Pinedale Assembly Center we had two center-
wide affairs. The first was a graduation ceremony for the
high school students who had been forced to leave school
prior to graduation. So close were they to finishing their
courses that full credit to graduate had been granted them.
An outdoor stand was built for the ceremony. I offered an
invocation, and a visiting clergyman (who he was and where
he was from, I am sorry to say I have completely forgotten)
gave an address.

Independence Day—Behind Barbed Wire
The Nisei insisted on celebrating Independence Day, even
though they were behind a barbed-wire fence, like criminals.
The *Pinedale Saw Dust* put out a special issue for which I

was asked to write a message. I would give anything to find
a copy of that issue! I was hard put to it by the request. What
could I, a Japanese, say to Japanese Americans who had
been virtually deprived of their citizenship rights and treated
by their own government exactly as if they were enemy
aliens? How hard pressed I was is evidenced by the fact that,
even to this day, I have not forgotten what I wrote in that
paper.

We dare celebrate the Fourth of July even in this place because
we complied with the evacuation order to show our patriotism
to this nation. Others are showing their patriotism in other ways.
Unfortunately ours had to take this form of expression. Nevertheless, our being here is no less an evidence of our loyalty to the
USA than going to war is with others. So it is as loyal citizens of
the USA that we are going to celebrate the Fourth of July. What
then should follow this celebration? What is our future as loyal
citizens of this great nation? Time will show what great things
are expected of us. Let us therefore take heed lest we should de-
teriorate while we are in this state of temporary custody.

I cannot remember whether we had any fireworks, but I
do remember that we had a wonderful day of athletic and
recreational events. In fact, that was by far the most mean-
ingful Fourth of July I have so far observed.

During this period I was twice given permission to leave
Pinedale. On the first occasion I was to accompany a woman,
whose daughter was a Sunday school pupil of mine, and her
husband to visit a relative at Sacramento State Mental Hospital. On arrival, the doctor told me the patient had been
suffering from dementia praecox, and I had a hard time ex-
plaining what this was to the woman and her husband. Subsequently the woman I accompanied had a fairly prolonged
period of depression, which fortunately did not become
chronic, but took up a lot of my time and energy as her pastor. Later I had to deal with no fewer than half a dozen individuals suffering from mental and emotional disorders,
none of them serious enough to require hospitalization.

They all, however, were indicative of the strains within the community.

On the other occasion I accompanied a family from Kent to Fresno County Hospital. Their oldest son, nineteen years old, was dying of leukemia. His life had been prolonged for about a week by blood transfusions, but eventually the doctors had to tell his parents that there was no hope for him. The difficult task of relaying that verdict in Japanese to his parents fell on me, as well as the task of comforting the dying youth. His was not the only funeral we had at Pinedale. There were others; and perhaps they would have died wherever they were. But the situation at Pinedale was such that the bereavement of one family became the bereavement of the whole community. Every time there was a funeral, the community spirit was intensified and solidified. People who had already parted with their worldly possessions were further reminded of the transitoriness of life itself. Death is always a sobering event; at Pinedale it was profoundly so.

Toward the end of July the group from California was transferred to the Poston Relocation Center in Arizona, and the announcement was made that those of us from Washington and Oregon were to be transferred to Tule Lake Relocation Center in northern California. When these announcements were made, the people from California were sorely disappointed. There was, in fact, much hue and cry on both sides that the groups were not being sent to the same place.

Making the Best of Our Situation

When we first arrived at Pinedale, we all thought that it would be our home for the duration, but no one liked it. To be sure, we were provided with three square meals every day, had a roof over our heads, and underwent no physical hardship except the wilting heat during the daytime. There was no forced labor, as there would have been in a concentration camp. In fact, there was no labor whatsoever. People suffered from idleness. Everybody wanted to leave the center and be on his own. Even old men found it hard to be so cooped up. Young men and women, born and educated in the United States, could not possibly take this kind of life for any prolonged period. Moreover, they all had rather happy images of American society and of American people. If they were not to be allowed to return to their homes, they were ready to go elsewhere, beyond the Rockies if necessary, where they could be free and could live by their own honest industry.

They were Japanese enough, at one moment, to want to maintain their kinship relations intact, but at another, they were American enough to be willing to leave their kinfolk and neighbors and go forth, even to unknown places, in order to be independent. I do not remember how many cases I personally pleaded before the administration, but the answer was always the same: "The WCCA cannot do anything about it." It became clear to us only after everything was over that the WCCA was an Army agency created solely to evacuate us, and the WRA was strictly a civilian agency created by the President's executive order to arrange and supervise our relocation. The WCCA was, therefore, the wrong tree to bark up if one wanted to be released from the camp.

Under normal circumstances, two months could hardly be time enough for people from such diverse backgrounds as those at the Pinedale Assembly Center to grow into an integrated community. But they did grow into an intimately solidified community, such as they might have been if they had been together for several generations. This happened not because anything was done by way of community development, but chiefly because of the dynamics of their situation. For one thing, they were forced to face their common predicament—namely, that because they were of Japanese descent, they were not really wanted by American society, at least by a sizable segment of it.

The sense of sharing the same destiny intensified their awareness of belonging to one another. Without exaggeration, they all felt that their day of doom had come. There could be no more future for them in America unless they were allowed to get out of camp. At this stage there was not much anti-American sentiment noticeable among them; neither was there much persecution complex. What was most pronounced was the sense of mutual belonging and of participation in a common destiny. The Pinedale Assembly Center thus quickly took on a group personality and became a remarkably integrated community.

There was, for example, no sign of moral disintegration to be seen all the time we were there, despite the fact that people had too much time on their hands. The days went by fast because people were engaged in one program or another. Individuals were quick to cooperate with one another to make their common life as tolerable as possible under the circumstances.

Church services, Scripture classes, and other religious functions, both Christian and Buddhist, were well attended. Cynics may say that that was because they had nothing else to do—which may be true. As for myself, I can only say that I preached some of my best sermons at Pinedale. The Bible study sessions on the Epistle to the Galatians which I gave once a week for six weeks can hardly be matched by any series I have given since. The instructions on the Apostles' Creed which I gave every Sunday evening could easily be the best interpretation of the Gospel I have given in my whole life. These, of course, are strictly subjective feelings about my own work, but from my many years' experience as a clergyman I know that I cannot be at my best when the congregation I am facing is not there trying to worship God in truth and in sincerity. That Japanese Christian congregation and I shared the awesome sense of standing before the Judgment Seat.

Almost everybody spoke rather openly of his frustrations and anxieties; nothing was bottled up. This was possible because, in broad outline, everybody had the same problem.

No one had to preface or footnote his remarks in order to
be clearly understood by others. No one pretended to have
no problems or to have all the problems of the world by himself. Former differences in wealth or social status were utterly irrelevant. All were thrust down to the same level, subjected to the same abominable meals, lack of privacy, dust
storms, and heat. Moreover, no one of us was responsible for
this state of affairs. We all were victims of an unknowable
force. The Pinedale Assembly Center was the kind of community that Moral Re-Armament tries to create but seldom
succeeds in producing. The reason an integrated community
emerged at Pinedale was that all lesser individual problems
were submerged by the one common problem—we were
people of Japanese descent.

Thus the center became a fantastically nice community to
live in, and people soon were resigned to staying there. Pinedale was no longer the name of a strange place. Although
they had been taken there without knowing where they were
going, the people quickly adjusted themselves to the place
after the initial shock of the heat, dust, and lack of comfort.
They were psychologically conditioned to making the best
of the situation. The result was that an amazingly sane community emerged. There is no way of telling how long this
happy state of affairs might have lasted if they had been allowed to stay on at Pinedale. I, for one, doubt very much
that it could have lasted much longer.

As we left Pinedale, Hauk, his eyes full of tears, shook
hands with every one of us as we passed through the gate.
Johns, King, and many others of the staff bid us good-bye.
I was able to say to each one of them, "I am glad to have
known you," and to mean what I said. I have not seen these
men since that day, but their faces, their voices, and their
characteristics still live vividly in my memory. My life has
been richer because I have them among my one-time associates; for associates they were to me, as I desperately tried
to minister to those people herded into Pinedale Assembly

Center; and I was an associate to them, I am sure, as they tried to run the center as best as they could. I owed nothing to them; they owed nothing to me. I was merely one of the evacuees, and they were appointed personnel of the WCCA. They were Americans and I was a Japanese. In 1942 that difference was enough to keep us far apart. But somehow we entered into a common venture that we took to our hearts, each in his own position. Our ultimate concern was to see that those several thousand people were adequately cared for physically, morally, and spiritually. Together we shared that task. I was genuinely glad that this sharing was possible and that they were the kind of people they were. I do not know where they are now, much less how to communicate with them. Nevertheless, I here pay my tribute to them.

6   A City Grows in the Wilderness

Once again I found myself on a train crowded with men, women, children—and luggage. Again the train windows were "blindfolded." I do not know the route we traveled, but it was long enough for us to spend the night on the train. When I woke up, it must have been around 5 A.M.; the train had already stopped. Presently we were told that we had arrived at our destination, Tule Lake. Another processing—family number, contents of luggage, etc., etc. Tired, sleepy, and uninspired by that prospect, I got off the train. Lo and behold, I was greeted by a hill overshadowing the camp, and beyond that hill was the snow-clad peak of Mount Shasta. I can never forget my emotions when I saw these, for almost unconsciously I mumbled to myself, "I will lift up mine eyes unto the hills; from whence cometh my help? My help cometh even from the Lord, who hath made heaven and earth."

I was following along with the crowd, when suddenly I was greeted by my good friend Andrew Kuroda, minister from Salem, Oregon. He, in immaculate clerical attire, and I, unshaven and in shirtsleeves and blue jeans, exchanged

hearty greetings, a meeting which was noted by Elmer Shirrell, Director of Tule Lake Relocation Center. Shirrell immediately took me aside, told me how glad he was to meet
me after having heard so much about me, and assigned me
a room (instead of sending me to the bachelor quarters). It
served as my quarters during my entire stay at Tule Lake.

Tule Lake Relocation Project

When our contingent arrived, people from sections of
Washington, Oregon, and California were already settled in,
and I found it more difficult to adjust myself. However,
there was no choice for me but to take what there was. When
the last expected group arrived, the total population of Tule
Lake reached approximately fifteen thousand. The camp was
officially designated Tule Lake Relocation Project and was
run by the WRA. At the head of the camp was the Project
Director, and we were called colonists. The official policy
was to discourage fraternization between colonists and appointed personnel, all of whom were Caucasian Americans;
for administrative purposes even Negroes were classified as
Caucasians.

Our camp, surrounded by sagebrush, was situated in the
middle of nowhere. The nearest town was Newell, California, a strong American Legion town from which we later
had a lot of trouble. In front of the camp, between the gate
and the hill, ran the highway connecting Klamath Falls, Oregon, and Reno, Nevada. Behind the hill was what little was
left of the old Tule Lake. In fact, the whole region was reclaimed land, a job which the German prisoners of World
War I had done. The ground on which our camp was built
was sandy and extremely hard on shoes. The whole camp was
divided into eight wards, each ward consisting of six blocks.
Members of the appointed personnel lived in barracks, better constructed than ours, on the other side of the administration building. Their area was set apart from ours by a
fence of barbed wire. The entire camp was wire-fenced and

had armed military personnel stationed just outside the gate.

I was initiated into the religious life of the camp at a Protestant ministers' meeting. There were seven or eight Methodists and one each from the Presbyterian, Baptist, Salvation Army, Independent, and Episcopal churches. My friend Kuroda and his friend (later to be mine also) the Rev. Shigeo Tanabe, from Sacramento, California, both Methodists, were the only young men; the rest were all elderly. It was quite evident that these two were the powers moving everything, and I joined them to complete a trinity. I was told that there was a barracks in each ward which could be used as a chapel and that while there was to be a Japanese-language service in each ward, there would be only three English-language services in the whole camp, to be taken care of by Kuroda, Tanabe, and myself. I was not released from taking the Japanese service for Ward VI either. On top of that, they put me in charge of the Sunday school, which had twelve hundred children and fifty or sixty teachers, with real possibilities of growing still bigger.

A Tense Encounter

Shortly after I arrived at Tule Lake, a small group of us were called in to meet a representative from the Office of War Information (or some such agency). The group was not in any sense an officially representative one. We had been hand-picked by the administration because we were considered to be influential in the community. The gist of the business was this: American prisoners of war were maltreated by the Japanese military. Would we be willing to broadcast to Japan, telling them how well we were being treated in the relocation center, so that the Japanese government might improve its treatment of the American prisoners of war?

Looking back, anyone can see how ridiculous that proposal was. In the first place, it presumed that we were also prisoners of war, something which the U.S. government repeatedly denied. The official argument to justify the mass evacuation of people of Japanese descent was the theory of protective custody. To turn around now and use us as if we were prisoners of war would be a gross contradiction. But we were in no position or frame of mind to argue such a point. Those assembled were silent for long, awkward minutes. And yet, this was America, and they could not possibly force any of us to broadcast to Japan, putting words prepared by others into our mouths. The whole thing had to be done democratically. So the argument was that if we had compassion on the Americans suffering as a result of maltreatment by the Japanese, we would be moved to render this humanitarian service in their interest.

The request was made, and we had to put our cards on the table. Those assembled, however, hardly knew one another. Some were Issei; some, Nisei. They were college professors, community leaders, clergymen, and the like. Each was worried about what others might have to say about any opinion he expressed, and no one quite dared to speak. The awkwardness soon turned into tenseness, and somebody had to break the ice. I decided to take that job on myself. I said, "We appreciate the humane treatment we have been receiving, both at the assembly center and at the relocation center. If, however, we were to broadcast to Japan, I would like to mention that in these centers there are American citizens as well as Japanese nationals." The implication of this statement, of course, was that we were not prisoners of war, although we were placed in a similar condition; and for such a condition the treatment accorded to us was fair and humane, except that bona fide U.S. citizens were being treated in exactly the same way as Japanese nationals.

My statement got the ball rolling. One of the group pointed out how in the assembly center they had to line up for an hour or so in the heat of the midday sun, only to get a couple of boiled potatoes and a piece of bread for lunch.

Another chimed in to tell a similar story about another assembly center. And when the group narrated the process through which people got there, the picture of the treatment the Japanese American was receiving in America was none too rosy. Lest the consideration become too one-sided, I ventured to point out that the kind of food that some had mentioned as having been served in some assembly centers was definitely below the standard of the average meals in America —but was far above that in Japan. "If the Japanese military gave American prisoners of war exactly the same kind of food which the Japanese soldiers were eating, without a speck of doubt Americans would scream a protest against it. From my observation in Japan over the past twenty years," I added, "Americans who go to Japan to stay, be they missionaries, scholars, diplomats, merchants, or tourists, continue to live as if they were in America, especially in terms of their eating habits. What is commonplace to average Americans is beyond the reach of the average Japanese. There is an unbridgeable gap in living standards between the two countries. Not that I intend to exonerate the Japanese military, but I wonder whether they might not be doing their best, though this is far from satisfying to Americans."

The conference ended without our committing ourselves to anything, and I thought the matter was closed. But a few weeks later I heard that the same issue was being discussed at the meeting of the Community Council and that the Council was split on the proposition. I was not invited to the Council, nor did many people seem to know anything about the informal conference that had been held earlier. As I remember, the Council finally voted against complying with the request of the OWI. The total effect of that proposal upon the Tule Lake community was, however, extremely unfortunate, and the incident was one of a chain of events that solidified Japanese evacuee opinion against the government.

The Organizational Pattern of the Center

A population of fifteen thousand makes a little city. Certainly the Tule Lake Project had all the problems of any city that size. How was it to be governed? The WRA followed the policy that this might be a training school for democratic living, specially designed for Americans of Japanese descent. At the same time, relocation centers were used as training centers for the would-be administrators of various phases of possible Allied occupation of Japan. At an early date a camp-wide election was to take place to choose members for a Community Council; only Nisei were eligible to vote and to hold office. From each ward several councilmen were to be elected. Issei were categorically eliminated, on the grounds that this was an American city and therefore could not be governed by a council in which an alien was included.

Election of the Tule Lake Community Council members took place uneventfully; afterward the Council was duly organized and elected Harry Mayeda, a young lawyer from Sacramento, as its chairman. The Council henceforth became the official spokesman for the entire Tule Lake community and its liaison with the administration. Let it be remembered that the Council was composed exclusively of Nisei, whose average age could not have been more than thirty, while the average age of Issei men was at least fifty-five. Where in the world was there a city, or even a little village, run entirely by young people aged thirty and under, without men and women of maturer years participating in its affairs? Tule Lake and the nine other relocation centers were just such abnormal communities, made that way by directives from Washington, which was so sensitive about aliens running affairs pertaining to the security of the United States.

The Issei did not raise a single voice in protest against the Council, but they paid no attention to it, either. To them the Council was no more than a bunch of youngsters, and that was that. If nothing had happened, the WRA could have reported to the Congress that even in the relocation centers the principle of Americanism was successfully upheld. However, the Council had to face a crisis very soon after its formation. As a background to this, the camp's operation must be explained.

Each block had a manager, a salaried position for which any person, Issei or Nisei, man or woman, could apply at the employment office. The administration was divided into various departments, such as personnel, maintenance, employment, social welfare, medical, farm, and school. The whole setup was patterned after an average city government, except that at Tule Lake the administration was entirely Caucasian, the city council was entirely Nisei, and the really dynamic part of the population was Issei.

In order to run the city smoothly and economically, the WRA had set up a work corps, open to any able-bodied evacuee, sixteen or over, willing to put in an honest day's work. Those accepted were assigned to various kinds of work essential to community life, and applicants could, of course, make their preferences known. They were compensated according to their work: about $19 a month for professional work, $16 for skilled work, and $12 for unskilled or menial work, plus clothing allowance for the worker and his dependents. It was stressed that these sums were not wages, but spending money over and above the room and board provided by the government. Those who did not want to work at all did not have to. Work of all kinds was available: on the farm, where they tried to raise enough food to feed the fifteen thousand at Tule Lake and still ship a surplus to other relocation centers; maintenance and construction, that is, plumbing, electrical work, carpentry, etc.; on kitchen crews, as cooks, waiters, dishwashers. As time went on, schools were opened and teachers were needed. In the interest of keeping up morale, all sorts of adult education classes and recreation projects were instituted, for which teachers and leaders also were needed. Offices needed stenographers and typists; the hospital needed nurses and nurse's aides. Pretty soon everybody was a member of the WRA work corps. People griped about the low pay scale, but in general they took the program with good humor. There was no move to demand a raise. Griping about the wages was more a pastime, and many had a jolly good time at it.

Thus, little by little, Tule Lake took on the character of a normal American community, and people began to behave as if they had always been there. With housing, no matter how crude; with work opportunity, no matter how little the compensation; with three square meals without fail; and, most important of all, with their families kept together, people soon began to feel settled in this community. They did not forget that the war was going on, that they had suffered tremendous economic loss, and that they were here as victims of the war. Far from forgetting, they were keenly aware of all that and, for that reason, believed that there could be no better place for them. With Japanese faces and Japanese names to identify them, where could they possibly be as safe as here in camp? They almost convinced themselves of the soundness of "protective custody."

The WRA, from its inception, had never intended to keep evacuees in camp for the duration. Its first director, Milton Eisenhower, and his successor, Dillon S. Myer, were both clear on that point. They conceived the task of the WRA to be that of helping the evacuees to resettle and join the normal stream of American society.

Director Shirrell of Tule Lake and his staff also understood their job to be that of keeping the evacuees as happy as possible, while they had to be there, and, at the same time, helping them prepare for ultimate resettlement outside the camp. They were guided in executing their policy by a basic sense of decency, fair play, and social justice; they wanted to make the community life at Tule Lake Relocation Center as nearly normal as possible, within the restrictions imposed on it. This was a well-nigh impossible objective, but Shirrell and his staff gallantly strove to achieve it.

The Fate of a Reasonable Proposal

While the relocation center began to take on the characteristics of a community, the people could not long remain a community of hermits. Montgomery Ward and Sears Roebuck began to do a tremendous mail order business. Barracks were beautified. Men, using scraps of lumber, built all sorts of furniture. Household goods that had been left behind were sent for. People began to come to church services in their Sunday clothes. Construction crews were busy building schools.

At this point two outstanding needs of the community were felt by those responsible for its welfare: consumer goods and leisure-time activities. To meet the first need, the WRA proposed to organize a consumers' cooperative. No more admirable step could have been taken. Although it took some time before the idea was fully accepted by the Community Council, it was finally approved and put into effect.

To meet the need for recreation, the WRA proposed the construction of a recreation hall which would be equipped to show movies. Quite unexpectedly, a furious protest was raised by the Issei community. The Nisei all supported the proposal, which made the Issei all the more furious. Many meetings were held, following which the Issei threatened the Community Council in no uncertain terms. The Christian clergy then met to discuss the matter. Most of the older men represented the view of the Issei in general. Their argument, in brief, was as follows: "The U.S. government has put us in this place. We have been deprived of all opportunity to make economic advance. They make us work for twelve, sixteen, or nineteen dollars a month. They have just set up canteens, and under the name of co-op encourage us to spend all the savings we accumulate. Now the proposal is to build a movie theater, and the Nisei are overwhelmingly

for it. What will be the consequences? Youngsters who do
not understand the whys and wherefores of the circumstances
will yield to temptations set up by the government and will
go to see movies every night. In no time, we Japanese as
a group will have lost every last penny we have earned by
our sweat." I was completely astounded at hearing otherwise
intelligent, level-headed Christian ministers argue along this
line. Obviously there was no use disputing with them at the
time.

Before the issue of the recreation center was settled, Bessie
Watanabe, whom we had left behind in Washington, died
of TB. Her mother, brother, and a close family friend requested me to go with them to her funeral. A special military permit was obtained, and a civilian guard was assigned
to us. His name was Dick Tracy, and he was an awfully
decent fellow. Though the occasion was an extremely sad
one, we nevertheless enjoyed breathing the fresh air of freedom for a few days and being back in Kent. While there,
Tracy allowed us to be pretty much on our own. The funeral service was conducted by the Rev. Dr. Arney, the re-
tired priest who had baptized Bessie; the Rev. Earl Schmei-
ser, then rector of St. John's Parish, West Seattle, who looked
after Bessie following my departure from Kent, and myself.
Some of her old friends were also there.

During my stay in Kent, I took the opportunity to call on
the mayor and the directors of the two banks. The mayor,
Maj. Richard Gooden, cordially received me and inquired
about many of the people in camp whom he knew. The
bank directors told me that the Japanese had paid all their
debts before leaving for the camp. They added how sorry
they were not to have the Japanese to deal with, for some of
those who replaced them were not nearly as trustworthy. We
stopped in a number of stores, where people received us as
if we had been there all the time. I was saddened, however,
to observe that our gardens, which used to be kept so neat
and orderly, were already showing the marks of neglect.

While the national government was crying for increased agricultural production, our former vegetable gardens were thick with weeds. Nevertheless, it was good to be among our old friends and neighbors and to be reassured of their friendship and confidence. The trip turned out to be the nicest gift Bessie could have given us on leaving her earthly home. It certainly helped me to stay sane for the ensuing ten months or more.

When I stepped back into the Tule Lake Relocation Center, I was immediately struck by the tension in the air. On the surface there was nothing unusual. People were moving about very much as they had before I left, but something made me feel that all was not well. When I reported to Director Shirrell, I asked him what had become of the recreation hall project. He said the Community Council had voted it down. There and then I told him that henceforth, when he had anything of importance to present to the Japanese, he should do so not only to the Community Council but also to a representative group of Issei; I would act as his interpreter. I suggested this because I was absolutely sure of his character and his motivation, and I was deeply concerned that such a genuinely good intention on his part had been so mercilessly distorted by the Japanese. The least I could do was to try to maintain the flow of communication between the administration and the colonists.

Thus the second crisis came and went—or so it seemed. But in fact the real crisis was in no way over. The incident of the abortive attempt to build a recreation hall was merely a symptom of the deep-seated ill health that manifested itself time and again in the community.

The Critical Distortion in Our Lives

Life at Tule Lake was largely regulated by bells. Each block had a large mess hall, where three meals a day were served to between two hundred and three hundred people and were announced by the mess-hall gongs. The cafeteria-style service tended to separate children from their parents. The youngsters usually were the first to hear the gong, and ran to the hall. They would sit with their playmates, eat what they liked and leave untouched what they didn't, and run out to play before their parents were even seated. Mealtime was the most important item on everybody's daily agenda.

Few people had any incentive for the "work" in which they were engaged. Japanese who had frequently been criticized by other Americans for working too hard, for too long, and for too little, thus undercutting unionized labor, became in the relocation center just as reluctant and indolent as the proverbial WPA worker of the 1930's. Issei and Nisei alike ceased to be the hard-working people they had been reputed to be. Having no incentive to work, they had no initiative to do anything for their own benefit, let alone for that of others. All creative imagination seemed to disappear. The whole situation was demoralizing, and increasingly so as time went by.

One of the indications of this demoralization was the trouble that repeatedly developed in connection with the meals. A daily menu was prepared by the central administration in accordance with sound dietary considerations, and much of the food had been raised on the farm. For every meal the necessary ingredients were delivered from the warehouse to each mess hall, together with the menu of the professional dietitian. In the absence of a trained cook, however, a group of amateurs took over the preparation of the meal. The result was sometimes surprisingly good, sometimes understandably bad, and most of the time mediocre. Actually, both in quality (that is, in terms of nutrition, not taste) and in quantity, the food at Tule Lake was not bad at all. I know for a fact that there were families who could not possibly have been used to meals half as good as those served there. Yet complaints about the food were increasingly raised from one block to another. The amateur cooks very quickly adopted the characteristic chef's temperament, so that complaints about food used to cause terrific commotion among the kitchen staff.

In view of these recurrent mess-hall crises, I decided to study the situation more or less analytically. I asked myself why people should complain so much about the food they were served. To find an answer, I did not take opinion polls or psychoanalyze anybody. I simply contemplated the whole situation, and found the answer in the breakdown of the family table and the absence of the family kitchen.

I have already alluded to the breakdown of the family table. It had further ramifications, however. Among other things, it meant that it was entirely possible for children, with the exception of infants, to spend all their waking hours without either seeing or being seen by their parents. When night came, they were all crammed into one room regardless of generation, age, or sex, as one family; but when morning came, everybody was on his own. There were not a few parents who seldom saw their own children during the day. This meant the breakdown of the family's sense of unity and solidarity. To children of tender age it meant the total lack of opportunity to receive parental care and instruction. The family table, under normal circumstances, is an institution around which the life of the family as a unit is centered. It is where children "eat and drink" their parents' love and care for them, as materially symbolized in the meals earned by the father and prepared by the mother. Even in a completely secularized family, the family table is a sacrament of parental love for children and of the intrinsic unity and solidarity of the family. This was the element completely missing from life in the relocation center. Children not only did not sit at table with their parents, where they would have learned manners and shared their day's experiences with other members of the family, but they also knew that what was before them had neither been earned by their father nor prepared by their mother.

The breakdown of the family table was, in fact, preceded by the absence of the family kitchen. In the relocation center a woman largely lost her functions as housewife and mother. As wife and mother, a woman prepares every meal for her family, within a budget based on the family income—which normally is what her husband earns—taking into consideration the likes and dislikes of all the members of the family; and she does all this without upsetting the nutritional balance required to keep everybody healthy. Under normal circumstances her role is taken for granted. Not even the woman herself is always conscious of it. In the relocation center she was no longer in charge of her family meals. Then, and only then, did it become clear, at least to me, what a work of art it is for her to prepare meals for her family every day of the week, every week of the year. It certainly tests her imagination and ingenuity. Without her wifely and motherly concern and love, she could not possibly do it. Looking at the same situation from the reverse side, what is set on the family table is nothing other than a visible and tangible sign of the invisible and imponderable love and care of her who is at the center of the family. The family table and family kitchen are thus sacramental means by which children feed on their parents' love and by which all the members grow together to solidify their mutual relationships. It is not so much the blood relationship or kinship as such that makes for family solidarity, but this business of growing together by feeding on one another's love! Such is the mystery of family life.

All this was completely lost in the relocation center. Children of all ages were quite aware that their parents were not earning their livings. Their bodies could be, and in fact were being, fed and otherwise cared for by someone else. The trouble, of course, was that their inner souls were not feeding on their parents' love and care, something no one else was able to supply. Worse yet, no one was giving thought to the problem. Adequate housing, balanced diet, sufficient clothing, some work to keep people's hands busy, schools to educate youngsters, and some leisure-time activities for all—what more could one expect from any government agency? Within the restrictions of the situation, the Tule Lake Relocation Center did admirably well—far better, in fact, than a public agency usually can—in meeting basic human needs. But the relocation center, by its very nature, had to be something of a collectivistic society, in which all lesser collectivities, including families, had to be subsumed. Herein lay the basic ill. I have never seen as clearly as I did at Tule Lake how tremendously important the family is for the healthy growth of every human being.

That very element was totally lacking at the relocation center. No wonder old and young alike complained about the food! No wonder cooks lost their tempers! No government agency, no matter how benevolent and enlightened, could make up for that deficiency. It was frequently maintained that Tule Lake was one big family, and in a sense that was true. But to the extent that it was true, the real families had to abrogate their respective sovereignty. Moreover, in the eyes of young children, their parents were definitely inferior to their grown-up brothers and sisters, who as U.S. citizens could elect and be elected members of the Community Council. For all these reasons many youngsters lost confidence in, and respect for, their parents. The loss of the family table and family kitchen was not simply a loss of opportunity to teach table manners to growing children, but a forceful symbol of the breakdown of that human institution which transmits moral and spiritual values from one generation to another. Man, indeed, does not live by bread alone.

7   Life in the Relocation Center

Readers may wonder what the women did to pass their time in the relocation center. That was something of an irony. Ever since they had arrived in the United States, many of them as "picture brides," most Issei women had had no time to enjoy themselves. They reared children, kept house, and helped their husbands in every way possible, day in and day out, year in and year out. To be sure, in many an instance, as wife and mother, the Issei woman had been the queen of the household. It was she who kept the growing family together, kept her husband's enterprise from falling apart, and kept the life of the household going within the limited means at her disposal. Her husband depended on her and her children adored her: in that she found both reward and satisfaction, and beyond that she sought no other glory. I have seldom seen such self-sacrificial life elsewhere.

The Issei Reactions to Camp Regimen

To such women life in a relocation center was really and truly a well-earned and highly deserved holiday. It meant liberation from lives of continuous drudgery. For the first time in their lives, they had something akin to free time in a substantial amount, and in many different ways they blossomed out. Most of them took employment of some kind with the work corps. Whether out on the farm or in the mess hall, in the hospital or administration building, the work was not too hard; moreover, they had the companionship of women from a similar situation and like background. Once the day's work was done, the rest of the time was completely at their disposal. There were English classes, classes in flower arrangement, sewing, and Japanese music, and all sorts of cultural things going on. They took advantage of these as rare treats they could not afford to let go by. When the schools were organized, they took active part in the PTA, in which, before the war, they had seldom been able to participate because of the language handicap and their confining domestic drudgery. Issei women thus unwittingly became the happiest people in the relocation center. They even began to look younger. Again unwittingly, they also prepared themselves for the new life which was to be theirs within a few years.

The Issei men in the relocation center, on the other hand, were the most badly affected of all. In the Japanese family, even in the United States, the man as husband and father was at once the breadwinner and the decision-maker for the entire family. In order to provide for them, he worked as hard as any mortal possibly could. In return, he commanded the respect of his wife and children and not infrequently demanded undisputed authority over them. He was always conscious of how dependent everybody was on him and of his ability to provide. In the relocation center, all this changed radically. The Issei man was just as much a ward of the government as his wife and children were. Their livelihood no longer depended on his earnings. No matter how hard he worked in the relocation center, he could not improve the living conditions of his family. Children were fully aware that he was no longer indispensable to them.

Thus the Japanese man in his mid-fifties or older, who

had spent all his life loaded with responsibility for his family and vested with authority over them, suddenly found himself stripped of both. In the old days, within the Japanese community, he had all sorts of civic and social functions to perform; he might have served, for example, on the board of directors of his local Japanese-language school. Segregated racially and restricted legally though they were, the Japanese in America had organized their society as well as any other group. Within the well-established structure of that community life, each man had a niche for himself and always enjoyed the sense of belonging, of being wanted, useful, and important. Now all that was completely lost to him. He began to feel how useless he was. He did not lose affection and concern for his loved ones, but a sense of futility overwhelmed him. To make matters worse, he could not hope for a future of his own in America.

In such a state of mind, the Issei man had little incentive to do anything. Too proud, he would not subject himself to learning English from young Nisei. Due to his nationality, he was barred from all political activities within the relocation center. He worked as a corps member primarily to kill time. PTA meetings were outside the scope of his concern as well as of his competence. Those who were religiously inclined, both Christian and Buddhist, found comfort in religious services. Others found consolation in gambling and drinking. Hard liquor was strictly prohibited in the relocation center, but it did not take very long before somebody made *sake* (rice wine) by fermenting rice. The fact that so many of these lost souls were there together made their state of affairs much worse.

Thus, the effect of life in the relocation center upon the Issei men was almost completely opposite to that upon the women. The men looked as if they had suddenly aged ten years. They lost the capacity to plan for their own futures, let alone those of their sons and daughters. It was indeed pathetic to see such moral and psychic (if not spiritual) de-

terioration develop. In one sense, it was more a matter
of morale than of morals. Gambling and drinking were
there, yes; but no immorality to speak of, say, in terms of
irregular sex relations. And yet this breakdown of morale
among Issei men could not remain exclusively their affair.
It soon pervaded all areas of camp life.

This deterioration made it exceedingly difficult to deal
with the Issei. They were moody. Nothing was satisfactory
to them. They lost their sense of reality. Facts were less important than what they imagined were facts. Their unceasing
complaints about food were symptomatic of this. They gob-
bled up all sorts of rumors, no matter how fantastic. Some
young people even started a game, trading on the gullibility
of the Issei community. They would plant a rumor at one
end of the center, then wait to see how fast it could travel
and how big it could swell by the time it reached the other
end.

Morale in the Schools

The schools came to reflect this low community morale.
Children did not show enthusiasm for, or interest in, school
work. Parents did not seem to care about it, either. The
place, of course, was not conducive to study, to begin with;
and the fact that they had to be there simply because they
were of Japanese descent made the children question
whether there would be any use for their education in
America at all. One result of their attitude was that the
teachers had some pretty touchy pupils to deal with. The
whole sweep of American history, from the aspirations of
the founding fathers to the fight against the racism and total-
itarianism of the Axis nations, took on a new slant when
taught in tar-paper shacks behind barbed-wire fences to
children who were, for the most part, American citizens.
Fortunately, however, we had eminently qualified and profoundly dedicated teachers to tackle that knotty problem.
There were also enough Nisei college graduates to assist
them—young people who were not only technically quali-

fied to teach school but also mature enough to see, in spirit, beyond the fences of their temporary confinement.

Shortly after the schools formally opened, the administration and the Community Council jointly sponsored a special morale-building week to help people see their life at Tule Lake in perspective. I was invited to speak for fifteen minutes on the meaning of education and to discuss whether the Nisei should devote themselves more to vocational-technical education than to general education. I spent hours preparing, for I felt the crucial importance that my message might have for the young audience. I can still remember quite distinctly what I finally said: "Vocational training, I do not say, is unimportant. As a means of livelihood you must have some skill, for which vocational education is indispensable. But more fundamental is a kind of general education that builds your character, which you need in order to live—the kind of education which will help to make a Gandhi of each of you, enabling you to think for yourself, to stand up for your convictions undaunted by any force, and to uphold the principles of justice, love, and peace against all odds."

I did not intend my speech to be a pious exhortation to youngsters who would not have an equal chance for employment and promotion in American society, but I definitely intended to challenge them to rise up some day to make *their America* greater than it then was. Whether my challenge had the desired effect is beside the point; the important thing is that after hours and hours of reflection and meditation, I felt constrained to speak as I did. I felt the occasion demanded that I raise the horizon of the Niseis' mental outlook far into the future, so that they might see their lot in the relocation center in proper perspective.

The Problems of the Nisei

At the relocation center, different age groups had different kinds of problems. There were some Nisei who were parents and whose children (Sansei) were, by and large, still infants, in kindergarten, or in the early grades of primary school. To the infants and youngsters of pre-discernment age the relocation center was something horribly different from what they had been accustomed to. Their reaction was best expressed by the frequently quoted statement of one six-year-old: "Mommy, let's go back to America." By and large, to that age group the crucial thing was, as is the case in every culture, to be with their mothers. Where their mothers were, there their homes were. Objectively, their problem was that, seeing their fathers and mothers in the kind of situation I have described, and without quite understanding what it was all about, they began to lose respect for their elders.

On the older children, relocation center life made an indelible impression on one score—the center was a place where Caucasian people governed and Japanese people were governed. Everything they saw, day in and day out, indicated that racial difference was identical with a caste distinction. They were all Americans, but those with white skin were, by virtue of their skin color, superior to those with colored skin. At Tule Lake it was singularly fortunate that Elmer Shirrell, the Project Director, and most of his key staff members were not only completely free from race prejudice but positively concerned about combating it where it existed. Furthermore, there were appreciable numbers of older Nisei mature and intelligent enough to see all the implications of race-caste identification. They worked together to keep that image of Tule Lake from becoming a permanent stereotype in the minds of the youngsters. The remarkable thing was that once the basic structure of community life was established, at least at Tule Lake, key members of the administration and a few Issei and Nisei in positions of leadership accepted each other as colleagues in a common venture. Washington might have frowned on that undue degree of fraternization, but at Tule Lake we were much more concerned about the job to be done than about such regulations. Social visiting between members of the appointed personnel and some of the evacuees soon became the accepted way for "shop talk" over a cup of coffee, a glass of beer, or some light refreshment—shop talk about how to make Tule Lake a better place for all involved. This kind of warm social intercourse, undergirding the working relationship between the administrative staff and the leaders of the evacuee community, created a social climate in Tule Lake without which hundreds of youngsters might conceivably have grown up with a deep-seated sense of inferiority based on race prejudice, coupled with a sense of hostility or even of vengeance toward Caucasian Americans.

The senior high school students were faced with their own peculiar problems. In addition to their basic education and vocational training, they were to learn how to be citizens in a free society, prospective homemakers, and parents. But how could they have a wholesome social life through which to get to know their peers of the opposite sex? Boys and girls whose interest in the opposite sex was duly awakened found themselves in an extremely awkward position. They wanted and needed privacy as well as some sort of guidance, if not supervision. In normal situations a boy and a girl are entertained in each other's home; and even when left alone by themselves, they are under the influence of their families. Their home embodies their cultural heritage of many generations, family codes of one kind or another, and acceptable standards of behavior. No elder needs to be physically present. The fact that they are allowed to entertain in their home makes them more than conscious of the part they must play as responsible members of society. Besides, the socially accepted patterns of dating, double-dating, and mixed-group activities are always governed within a given society by a certain code of behavior.

Such a basic structure of mores was completely lacking in the relocation center, the city put together literally over-

night in a God-forsaken desert. Tradition-bound though
the Japanese were, when abruptly uprooted, they were not
able to bring with them much of their cherished cultural
heritage. Under the false pretense of being one big family,
they were compelled to endure an almost absolute absence
of privacy, which resulted in the relocation center's becoming an aggregation of disgruntled and unrelated individuals.
Indeed, all manners seemed to have been left behind when
they entered the center. We witnessed, soon after we were
settled, heartrending scenes created by a people who had
always been known for their social etiquette, graciousness,
courtesy, and decency. Except for the beds, the rooms were
absolutely bare when we were first assigned to them. When
it was announced that scrap lumber was available, the fights
over those miserable boards between previously close friends
and neighbors were really something. Where were their
manners, their sense of mutual respect and courtesy, so characteristic of Japanese people? All those finer things of life
apparently were left behind, along with the excess baggage.

In this sort of society, if one could still call it a society,
how could adolescents learn to fall in love, court, marry, and
make a home according to the way of a civilized people? In
order to enjoy the desired and necessary privacy, youngsters
had to run away from other people—friends, neighbors,
parents. They could not find one spot under the sun, so they
felt, where they could be just with each other, without of-
fending somebody or without becoming an object of scan-
dalous talk. So they had to go out of bounds, as it were, to
win a little privacy. Should some of these youngsters have
made irremediable mistakes in such a situation, who could
blame them? Growing pains are difficult enough under the
most favorable circumstances, and for even the most carefully reared children. It is, without exaggeration, little short
of a miracle that there were not ten times as many cases of
juvenile delinquency as there actually were.

Of the young adults, some were already married, some

about to be married, and others single. Many were waiting to be allowed to go to colleges and universities in non-military zones. Some were already out of college and wondering what to do with themselves. Men of military age who had not been drafted prior to the evacuation order were without exception reclassified as "enemy aliens." Here they all were, able-bodied and willing to serve their country, yet kept within the confines of the camp. They were the most disappointed, dismayed, and frustrated of all.

On the other hand, the Issei, once so frightened and dependent on their sons and daughters, became increasingly bold and dared to say: "Where is your U.S. citizenship? What good is it doing you? Isn't your government treating you exactly as it is treating us enemy aliens? Do you still think it necessary to follow the direction of your government? Is it not high time for you to wake up to the fact that to the U.S. government you are nothing but Japanese, just as DeWitt clearly stated: 'Once a Jap, always a Jap'? Don't be so silly as to side with the WRA and establish all sorts of rules and regulations over us. Make up your minds to be good Japanese and come along with us." The only saving factor in this connection was the language barrier between Issei and Nisei, which kept these ideas in the minds of many old Issei from being adequately communicated to the young Nisei. But there is no denying that privately and publicly the Issei constantly pressed this line of argument on the Nisei.

The Alienated Kibei

There was one group in the camp peculiar to itself, and commonly known among Japanese Americans as Kibei. They had been born in the United States, and after having been sent to Japan for their education, had returned to America. (*Ki-bei* literally means "returning to America.") Both men and women were in this category, but it was the men who caused the problems at the center. Because their parents had thought it better that they be brought up more as Japanese than as Americans, they had attended primary and secondary schools in Japan. Some of them were fortunate enough to have had uncles or aunts or grandparents who were intelligent and understanding enough to be their temporary foster parents. Many, however, had suffered from a lack of proper parental care and supervision during the most impressionable period of their lives. Furthermore, most of them had attended the Japanese schools at the height of Japanese imperialistic militarism. Upon returning to the United States after graduation from secondary schools, many Kibei youths found themselves misfits among both the Issei and the Nisei, let alone among Americans in general. In fanatic pro-Japanese outlook, they outdid everyone. Although they craved social intercourse with their own age group, the Nisei turned up their noses at them as being "too Japanese," for they spoke English poorly and with a characteristically Japanese accent, and they behaved more like Japanese in Japan.

Until the evacuation finally took place, Kibei youth as a group were more under suspicion than either the Issei or Nisei, simply because they were U.S. citizens and had had thoroughgoing Japanese education. They knew it, too, and therefore were very cautious. In the relocation center they felt emancipated, yet many of them were misfits. To them the Issei were nothing but old fogies, while the Nisei were less than half-baked Japanese who, incapable of standing on their own, were kowtowing to the U.S. government or the white race. Numerically the Kibei were a minority who, for good or for ill, were now on U.S. soil. Aware that they were not very well accepted by Americans in general and did not fit into any segment of the Japanese-American community, the Kibei youths became either timid introverts or belligerent troublemakers, suffering in both cases from deep-seated inferiority complexes. This, of course, was the plight of the Kibei youth as a group, but not of every individual Kibei youth. There were appreciable numbers of them who were sufficiently "men of two cultures" and as such were destined to make many positive contributions by both enriching the American culture and bridging the chasm between the Japanese-American community and the rest of American society.

The Core Problem

The relocation center community was thus in an explosive condition. Nothing, no matter how good in its own right, was good enough to please everybody in the camp. We had one strike after another: kitchen crews, coal workers, construction crews, farm workers. No one knew what was going to happen from day to day.

I first discussed the sociopsychological state of Tule Lake with young Ted Waller, then in charge of community activities and recreation. (He subsequently enlisted in the Army and left his post at Tule Lake, which was filled by another excellent man, Corliss Carter.) One day Ted told me that visiting the center was a Professor Robert Redfield of the University of Chicago, in whom I could place my absolute confidence and to whom I should unburden myself with regard to the Tule Lake community. Dr. Redfield, noted social anthropologist, was giving his services to the WRA as a technical consultant. I do not remember what I told him in that interview, except that, in my opinion, it was absolutely unnatural, as well as ridiculous, to expect the Tule Lake community to be peaceably and orderly governed without having the Issei officially participate in the Community Council. U.S. citizenship laws notwithstanding, such a state of affairs was downright against human nature, if not sociological principles. Some weeks later there was another visitor, a Dr. Sweet from the Community Analysis Section of the WRA, who told us that the WRA was going to set up an advisory council, consisting of Issei, to assist the Community Council, and that at the same time there was to be one community analyst appointed to each of the ten relocation centers.

I do not now remember exactly when the Planning Board was established or when Professor Marvin Opler, of Reed College, Portland, Oregon, came to Tule Lake as its community analyst. "Planning Board" was the name given to the advisory council consisting of one Issei elected from each of the eight wards. I was elected from Ward VI and served as a member of the Planning Board until Tule Lake ceased to be a relocation center. It was gratifying, at least to some of us, to note that the WRA was, at the top policy-making level, trying to cope better with the complex situation of the relocation center.

The establishment of the Planning Board gave to the Issei a channel through which their voices could be heard in matters pertaining to the well-being of the community, although legally they had no rights whatsoever. At Tule Lake, however, unusually fine men were elected to serve as the executive committee of the Board, in whom the Community Council placed profound confidence, so that the Planning Board virtually became something of a privy council to the Community Council. There was an accident of history in that situation, too. The chairman of the Community Council, Harry Mayeda, and I, the youngest member of the executive committee of the Planning Board, happened to be of about the same age, and struck up a friendship which has lasted until this day. My chief function was that of interpreter. Negotiation between the administration and the evacuee community was always extremely difficult because of the language barrier, and the Community Council, being exclusively Nisei, could not help very much. Consequently, in the interest of the full and smooth flow of communication all around, the Planning Board and the Community Council met jointly whenever anything of importance confronted the community. Henceforth all appeals to, and negotiations with, the administration were done by representatives of the two bodies. At last the Issei and the Nisei were able to cooperate with each other.

Autumn Arrives

Community life at Tule Lake was such that a daily routine was more or less established for every member. The month of August slipped by before we knew it. On Labor Day we had an outdoor ceremony at which Elmer Shirrell spoke. I remember the occasion for a number of reasons. First, the ceremony was held under a blazing sun so strong that one of the little fellows in a Boy Scout uniform fainted right in front of the speakers' platform. Second, the young fellow who presided at the ceremony, a complete greenhorn at public speaking, was shaking like a tree in a storm. Third, it was the first time I interpreted for Elmer Shirrell. My job was made more difficult than usual, inasmuch as Shirrell quoted from the sermon he had heard me preach the day before. When the interpreter says "I," he does not mean himself; but when his own words are quoted in the speech he is translating, and especially when he is a greenhorn at it, it tends to become complicated.

The region where Tule Lake is located, the northern part of California near the Oregon border, is blessed with a very nice climate. I do not remember the altitude, but the air was always crisp. Even in the midst of summer it was cool in the morning, and at sundown the air immediately turned cool again. During the heat of the day the breeze was so refreshing that in the shade one did not suffer from heat at all. It seldom rained.

The center was surrounded by a sea of sagebrush, in the midst of which were little mountains standing out like islands. When life at the center was more or less organized, the administration announced that the hill right outside the gate was no longer out of bounds. That hill became a favorite spot for ever so many of us, although it was rocky and terribly steep. From the top, one could see the residue of the old Tule Lake. And in the distance one could always see snow-clad Mount Shasta, standing as if to remind us of eternity and giving new meaning to our daily life.

Soon it was autumn, and what a gorgeous sky we had over us, especially in the evening, when the west was burning red and thousands of geese flew above in perfect formations! As the sinking sun left in shadow every stone and twig on the ground, the faces of the children glowed as they watched the sky, the clouds, and the geese that came and went. How many times I stood alone there in awe and ecstasy, completely absorbed in the quiet of the dusk and telling myself how wonderful it was to be alive! Was that an evasion of reality—cold, disagreeable, and distasteful reality? A momentary flight into a world of fantasy and unreality? Say what you will about it, I still cherish those blissful moments. It was those moments of serenity that helped me to keep going from early morning till late at night, dealing with every conceivable kind of human problem, seven days a week for nearly a year.

What a contrast—Nature and human nature, as I saw them at Tule Lake! That God-forsaken place, in the midst of miles and miles of sagebrush, was not forsaken by God at all. From time immemorial old Tule Lake had been Nature's reserve for the migratory fowl to rest on their journeys between Canada and Mexico. But what an ugly sight, the rows and rows of tar-paper barracks, surrounded by barbed-wire fences and watched by armed guards day and night! The place was a symbol of hatred and jealousy, inner conflict and enmity, that got the better of humanity— a symbol of what the Bible calls the wages of sin. And the fifteen thousand of us who were confined there were by no means free from those black things that characterized humanity at large, as my story will presently show. Indeed, it is no exaggeration at all when I say that there I saw humanity at its best and at its worst. And I saw it not as a spectator, but as one intensely involved in it—saw it from within and experienced it as a tangible reality.

8 The WRA Resettlement Proposal

During the period that I have been describing, the WRA had been working out in Washington a plan whereby evacuated Japanese Americans and Japanese could be relocated as soon as possible. The relocation would be in areas other than where their homes had been and where they rightfully belonged. This plan contrasted sharply, however, with the thinking of the evacuees. As they saw it, the U.S. government was spending millions of dollars to maintain the ten relocation centers—an expenditure that made sense only if the evacuees were to be interned at these centers for the duration. What national government, they reasoned, would go to such an expenditure merely to make enemy aliens comfortable for a temporary stay? And so people settled down in the center and planned their lives accordingly, for there were countless little things which, unless well planned, could make daily life really miserable. Moreover, little seemed to be heard of their desire to be released from the centers.

Student Relocation
Just about the time when most of the evacuees had reached this state of mind, the plan on which the WRA had been

working was announced, and those who wanted to leave the relocation centers were advised to put in their applications. At first the announcement was not too disturbing, for those who were really eager to be released from the camp were mainly college students. Most of them slipped away without making any public announcement, so that few outside of their immediate families knew that they had gone. In due time, however, the number of such students was sizable, and their parents naturally became anxious about their safety.

Student relocation was a story in itself. When the order for mass evacuation had been issued and it had become clear that Nisei college students' studies were to be interrupted, the American Friends' Service Committee spearheaded the organization of the Student Relocation Council, which had the sanction of the federal government. The Council worked untiringly to interest colleges and universities outside of the military zones in accepting Nisei students from colleges and universities on the Pacific Coast. This, of course, entailed many cumbersome and delicate problems, such as the transfer of credits between colleges having somewhat different credit systems. Another problem was public sentiment toward the Nisei in the community in which a given college was located. Not a few midwestern and eastern college towns put up unbelievably tough opposition to having a few Nisei students admitted into their midst. Some colleges were extremely adamant, at least at first, in refusing to accept Nisei. To be admitted into a college with an Army/Navy Specialized Training Program, Nisei students had to be cleared by the FBI and the Army and Navy Intelligence Services. And, finally, there were the problems of those who were being transferred to state universities with state residence requirements, and of many others who needed scholarship aid.

The Student Relocation Council literally combed the institutions of higher learning all over the United States and negotiated with hundreds of them, besides appealing for scholarship aid to sponsoring colleges. At the same time, the government agencies had to be worked on to facilitate the process of transfer. Furthermore, once the mass evacuation had taken place and college students were settled with their parents in the relocation centers, many parents became increasingly hesitant about letting their sons and daughters go to unknown schools in strange cities. Not infrequently, students had lost all incentive to continue their college education.

Leave for Seasonal Work

After the Nisei college students left, there appeared another disturbing development. In the face of the labor shortage, big farm operators in Washington, Oregon, Idaho, Montana, and even farther east approached the WRA, seeking evacuees to work for them. I do not know what sort of negotiations took place before those farm operators, sugar beet producers, canning companies, and others finally sent their agents to the relocation center to recruit labor; neither do I know whether it was the WRA that approached the prospective employers or vice versa. One can be sure that there must have been a lot of discussing, clearing, and processing by the FBI, the Farm Security Administration, the WRA, and the town fathers of the local communities before the recruiting agents were finally allowed to come to the center. It was to the credit of the WRA that scrupulous care was taken to protect evacuee labor from being exploited. Those who went out on contract were paid according to the prevailing wage scale, with no discrimination against them being tolerated.

The first who ventured to go out on contract for seasonal work were, as might have been expected, the young men, predominantly Nisei. Issei, because of their status as enemy nationals, found it more difficult to obtain permits, and were not a little fearful to go out. Moreover, once settled in the camp, they were extremely reluctant to move again. To the youthful and vigorous Nisei, the situation looked different. Both the money they would earn and the freedom from confinement they would experience were strong attractions. Consequently, many Nisei applied for seasonal work, and once out, they had no wish to return to the center. The so-called seasonal leave permit could be extended, if the party involved so desired and it was not objectionable to the WRA.

Both the students who departed and the young men who went out to work as farmhands caused no small concern to the Issei, to whom the image of American society had become increasingly remote. The relocation center had become, for the Issei, an island separating them from the hostility of society. This sense of security—or, more precisely, pseudo security—was rudely shaken. The young people who had left, restored their contact with the outside world.

The Effects of Internment

It was not until about ten months later (August, 1943), as a result of a two months' trip outside, that I became painfully aware how morbid a society the Tule Lake Relocation Center was, although I had been quite conscious of its moving in that direction as early as September or October, 1942. The relocation center, having been quite artificially and suddenly brought into being, had rapidly turned into as closed a society as a primitive tribal community. The evacuees had been involuntarily closed in to begin with, but they themselves soon closed both the gates and the windows of their minds as well—an ostrichlike community indeed.

The morbidity of this society manifested itself in several distinct ways. First, the community was increasingly dominated by the Issei, without a change in its political structure. The Planning Board overshadowed the Community Council. Second, the mental frame of reference of the Issei centered more and more on Japan as time went on. They appeared to be deliberately trying to forget what had happened to them in the immediate past and to look forward again to their retirement to Japan. The Issei had transferred themselves to a world of fantasy. Distant past and remote future became more real to them than the immediate past and the immediate future, or even the present. Third, and concomitant with the second, for the Issei, American society lost its reality. The fence that enclosed them became an impenetrable wall which set them apart from that society, which to them became virtually a distant land—alien, unknown, and unknowable. No wonder they were rumor-prone!

In those days the Issei found the greatest satisfaction in the war news, factual and fictitious alike, that was favorable to Japan. If one had added up the number of U.S. battleships which the Japanese Navy was reported to have destroyed, it would certainly have been several times as large as the total number the U.S. Navy actually had. Every day some unidentified Issei within the center was reported to have heard over his short-wave radio (which he had reportedly smuggled in) that so-and-so many U.S. ships had been destroyed by the Japanese Navy. Such "news" spread like wildfire from one corner of the camp to the other, with few Issei questioning its validity. When the U.S. press and radio reported differently, the report was rejected as a distortion of fact for propaganda purposes. They were indeed living in a fool's paradise.

Such a sociopsychological climate inclined religious people all the more to religious preoccupations. In the Pinedale Assembly Center the mood of the Issei Christian group had been genuinely forward-looking, whereas at Tule Lake their mood was more otherworldly, in the sense of escaping the harsh reality of the here and now. Also profoundly significant was the revival of interest in Buddhism on the part of a great number of non-Christian Issei who until then had been almost completely indifferent to religion. This was not at all unnatural, for, as both their distant past (childhood in the now idealized old Japan) and their remote future (retirement in the new glorified Japan) took on greater reality than their immediate past and present, their preoccupation turned from the business of earning a livelihood and building up economic security to religious matters. But since they had been indifferent to religion, the only religion they could think of or turn to was that which they had known as the religion of their family. And now, of course, their whole mental frame of reference was Japan, so it was unthinkable for them to turn to Christianity. Buddhist services came to be very well attended, and the Issei's viewpoint became more and more backward-looking and otherworldly.

To people in such a collective state of mind, both student relocation and seasonal work leave came as a terrible shock that acted like a poison in their systems. The Issei community began to manifest all the symptoms of depressive paranoia and persecution complex. First, they lamented the "facts" that the hostile world would not leave them alone and that, in order to persecute them, that world was luring their loved sons and daughters away from them.

No one, of course, expressed his feelings in such words. Their way of expressing it was to indulge in the mysterious fascination of rumoring—telling and believing rumors about their children. The most prevalent rumors pertained to the mistreatment which Nisei had presumably undergone when they left the center. To be sure, there were not a few cafés and restaurants that refused to serve Nisei; neither was it at all surprising if there were some Americans who showed prejudice toward them. There certainly were unpleasant incidents both before and after the mass evacuation, but in the fall of 1942 there were amazingly few incidents of the sort. And yet the Tule Lake Center was full of "reports," "accounts of eye witnesses," and "gossipings" about so-and-so's daughter having been attacked, about so-and-so's son having been thrown out of a restaurant, and about such-and-such a town objecting to the Nisei being employed by the leading industry of the area. Judged by the rumors rampant in the camp, American people were nothing but atrocious savages, always standing ready to prey on the poor Japanese Americans. It was amazing how quickly a stereotyped image of Americans developed among the Japanese in the relocation center, an image that in its detail was just as atrocious as the stereotyped image of Japanese then prevalent among the American masses. Individual Americans who used to be their neighbors, customers, and friends were somehow forgotten, and all Americans were put in one category—anti-Japanese.

Another Shock

There was yet another upset in store for our closed community. Some time in the fall, representatives from the personnel procurement office of the U.S. Army Military Intelligence Service Language School (MISLS) arrived at Tule Lake to recruit volunteers from among the Nisei men of draft age. No effort had been made to prepare the Japanese community for this visit, and it came as a great shock. It also made clear that the WRA policy-makers did not understand the rapidly deteriorating collective psychology of the Issei community.

The recruiters carefully explained that the war in the Pacific had reached the stage where the Army needed Japanese linguists in large numbers and as quickly as possible. Where but among the Nisei, they asked, could they find candidates with such highly specialized linguistic qualifications? Thus an appeal was made to the Nisei as patriotic citizens of the United States, their temporary status in the relocation center notwithstanding.

To the Issei this appeal had no basis in justice—it was downright dirty, crooked, dishonest, and even cowardly.

It was one thing to send their sons to fight the Germans, but entirely another to send them to the Pacific to fight the Japanese. How could they face their relatives here on earth and their ancestors hereafter? This had been the one thing that they dreaded when war broke out between the United States and Japan, and that they thought they had been spared when they were herded into the camps.

The Nisei looked at the matter from an entirely different point of view. Of course they were hard put to it to make up their minds, but it at least offered them a new opportunity, heretofore closed to them, to demonstrate their loyalty to their country in a much more positive way than by mere compliance with the evacuation order. Furthermore, many of the older Nisei, mature in their thinking and having had some experience of making their living in American society, were convinced of two things in connection with this war. One was that war against Hitler was not only in Europe but just as much in the United States, of which their own plight as evacuees was the most eloquent evidence. The other thing was that, should the Allies lose this war, there would not be the ghost of a chance for democracy to survive. The Nisei were more profoundly aware of that than were most other Americans, chiefly because of their insight into the state of affairs in Japan, which they had gained, however indirectly, from their parents.

Amazingly large numbers of Nisei volunteered, most of them against the express will of their parents. Some acted secretly; some after several days and nights of bitter argument with their parents. When the showdown came, the parents had to give in, for the U.S. law clearly states that anyone who deliberately interferes with a U.S citizen's execution of his military duty is guilty of treason (or something to this effect). Parents therefore could go only so far in trying to dissuade their sons from volunteering for military service; and if the son made up his mind to do so, they could no longer make any effort to persuade him to change his mind. This, of course, embittered the Issei all the more.

I remember the send-off party that was held for the volunteers, with their parents and friends present. Elmer Shirrell spoke, and it was a difficult job for me to interpret for him that day. The whole atmosphere was entirely different from that at the send-off parties in Kent. People were under tension and restraint; there was not a shred of gaiety. With everybody saying the right things at the right moment, the program was carried out in perfect order. Soon after the party, the volunteers left for their special training at Camp Savage, Minnesota.

The departure of a sizable number of Nisei as volunteers to the MISLS left both a big hole in the Nisei group and a deep emotional wound in the Issei community, a wound that it was going to take a long, long time to heal. We lost a good number of Sunday school teachers, youth work leaders, recreation and leisure-time activity leaders, and some Community Council members. The cream of the older Nisei group seemed to have been snatched away. In my position as a pastor, I began to find an increasing number of Issei parents, especially fathers, growing despondent, for they thought that now that the Nisei had "turned against Japan," they could no longer return to Japan and face their relatives. Behind that despondency was an irreconcilable bitterness. However, few people were aware of its existence, for the Issei had not lost their capacity to suppress their feelings.

The Year Draws to a Close

Thanksgiving Day, 1943, at Tule Lake was a gala affair, with the bounty from its own farm—the farm which had been made out of the wilderness. A civic service was held at which Mrs. Mary Farquarson, State Senator of Washington, happened to be present. The only thing that stands out in my memory of this service is that Noboru Honda, a distinguished leader of the Buddhist group at Tule Lake and a member of the Community Council, read Psalm 23, and read it beautifully. Christians and Buddhists, Issei and Nisei, Caucasian and Japanese, WRA personnel and evacuees, participated, and the service was as close to the ancient agricultural festival as any Thanksgiving Day I had ever celebrated. When the previously barren soil brings forth the fruits of the earth, however it may have happened, man cannot help rejoicing. For one day we forgot all our troubles and were thankful to be alive.

Soon the geese were no longer in the sky, and winter set in to stay. Those of us connected with the Sunday school began to be concerned about Christmas programs for the children and the problem of Christmas presents for them. In the middle of nowhere, how could one get enough of anything to meet the needs of several thousand children? We hated to see children go without a Christmas present, this Christmas especially!

By the middle of December, however, the warehouse at Tule Lake was filled with all sorts of packages, large and small—Christmas remembrances sent to the children by countless church and civic groups throughout the country in response to an appeal made by the newly created Committee on Resettlement of Japanese Americans of the Federal Council of Churches. Every child, Christian and non-Christian alike, had a Christmas present. Those gifts sent to relocation centers were indeed more than just toys or books. They were carriers of good will from American men, women, and children to the adults and children of Japanese descent who were confined in the relocation centers. Few people were as painfully aware as I how badly the Japanese were in need of some such visible sign of good will toward them from the American people at that time. Without such a reassurance, many of them might have gone completely to pieces.

The Tule Lake Relocation Center was thus at ease, so to speak, when the old year slipped into the past, and a new year was ushered in while a midnight watch service was held by the flickering light of candles. There were no church bells to herald the coming of the new year there. But to the Issei, even after so many decades away from their old country, New Year's Day was still the biggest and most important festival of all. They made the most of it, returning thanks to God for having brought them to the beginning of a new year and petitioning him that this new year might turn out to be better than the one just ended.

This is no place for eulogy, nor am I in the position to make an objective evaluation of Elmer Shirrell's administration. I can neither praise him nor criticize him. I can, however, honestly say that it was to his credit that a number of near explosions were averted. For this he did not have any magic formula, nor did he use tricks of the administrative trade. He was an honest man, and trusted people for no other reason than that they were people. When I volunteered to be his interpreter and placed myself at his disposal, he accepted me with no ifs or buts. An offer genuinely made was genuinely accepted; he never wondered for one moment whether I had an axe to grind or ulterior motives. Before I left his office, he said to me, "If you're willing, I'll hold biweekly public meetings, to which all members of the Planning Board and the Community Council, and anybody else interested, will be invited. There I'll explain the WRA policy on various matters and answer any questions from the floor. I hope by this means that our problem of communication can be licked." I of course agreed. From then on, every other Wednesday or Thursday evening was reserved for the open meeting, which people eagerly looked forward to attending. As this kind of encounter was repeated, people came to see that Elmer Shirrell did not hold back anything of public significance and that he essentially trusted them. Though not all the things he did pleased everybody, toward the end of his administration the people at Tule Lake were thoroughly convinced that he was their friend. He was quite amused when he learned that the old Issei people were referring to him as the Father of Tule Lake.

The behavior and outlook of many of his administrative staff reflected Shirrell's conviction and principle with regard to the evacuees. They of course did not turn Tule Lake into a paradise, but beyond the shadow of a doubt they restored genuine human relationships between two groups of Americans once artificially separated by racial differences. They accomplished this against tremendous odds. No fancy-sounding technique expounded by race-relations experts would have done it while the kind of collective psychology prevailing in Tule Lake was at work. Elmer Shirrell, his wife Eleanor, and a majority of the senior members of the administrative staff trusted us, unassumingly and as a matter of course, and we all responded to them with the same kind of trust. We were indeed sad to see the Shirrells go.

9 The Loyalty Registration Crisis

Elmer Shirrell was succeeded as director by Harvey M. Coverley, who continued Shirrell's tradition of bi-weekly open meetings, at which I continued to serve as interpreter. At the first meeting he announced that the latest policy of the WRA was to liquidate the relocation centers as fast as possible and that he was there to help facilitate that process. He meant this to be the happiest possible news to the evacuees—the "Gospel of release to the captives"—and expected a joyous response from his audience. Instead he got a cold silence and anxious looks. Coverley, as I came to know him, was an extremely honest and just man. He had no ill will or bad intentions, but he was also a man who followed directives from above to the letter. One always knew exactly where he stood, what he meant, and how one stood with him. But he obviously was not the man to handle people in a complex and morbid state of collective mind.

A few weeks later, without warning, the new WRA program was announced. This was the program which later came to be called the loyalty registration program. Once announced, it was destined to explode like a time bomb, in a way that made the whole situation even more difficult to handle.

Who worked out the program I do not know, though it cannot be doubted that the WRA, the Army, and the JACL all had some part in it. At any rate, the program was intended to solve all the knotty problems at one stroke. The Army, supported by the JACL, was to organize an all-Nisei combat team to be sent to the European Theater of Operations. Volunteers were to be solicited from among the Nisei in the relocation centers as well as from among those who by then had been transferred to colleges and universities or otherwise relocated. At the same time, the WRA was to conduct a mass registration of all evacuees—Issei and Nisei, men and women—who were in the relocation centers, and to place on record each person's attitude toward the United States.

The Notorious Questionnaire

Thus there were two distinct programs simultaneously presented, one sponsored by the Army and the other by the WRA. In the WRA program, every person of age was required to fill out, in secret, a questionnaire. By then we had become accustomed to filling out all sorts of forms and questionnaires, to being fingerprinted, and to signing documents. This time, however, the form had two questions on it which terribly upset the Issei. Those questions read something like this:

(a) Do you pledge your loyalty to the government of the United States and promise to abide by the laws of this country? Answer Yes or No.

(b) Do you forswear your allegiance to the Emperor of Japan? Answer Yes or No.

The form was distributed through the offices of the block managers, where each person was to come to fill out his form in secret, as if casting a ballot in an election. WRA expected to get this job done in a day or two, but very few Issei registered. One day, two days went by, and nothing much happened.

Issei Reactions

Among the Issei a heated debate was going on day and night as to whether they should register at all. Some of us, upon finding out what the questions were, immediately pointed out to the administration how unfair the second question was to the Issei, for to answer No to it would have made them categorically disloyal to the United States, while to answer Yes would have made them virtually men without a country. We strongly advised the WRA to drop that question from the form to be filled out by the Issei. The Project Director of Tule Lake had no authority to alter the questionnaire without directive from Washington, and no immediate decision was made. In the meantime, the Issei requested a mass meeting at which they might discuss how they were to answer these two questions, but their request was flatly refused, a refusal that they could not understand. To allow them to meet, however, would have been to defeat the purpose of this program entirely, from the standpoint of the WRA. I publicly stated that as an Issei, I would answer Yes to the first question and No to the second; and, if this did not please the WRA, that would be the WRA's business, not mine. As long as I was in the United States and was receiving benefits of law and order from the U.S. government, I would conscientiously pledge my loyalty to the government. But as long as the law of the United States prohibited me, as an Asian, from applying to be naturalized as a U.S. citizen, I would unequivocally answer No to forswearing my allegiance to my own country. Such a rational explanation, however, fell mostly on deaf ears, for the Issei by and large were completely alarmed by this move, which they saw as a new device of the WRA to persecute them. Several days later a directive from Washington arrived, eliminating that knotty question from the form to be answered by the

Issei, but it was too late. In the minds of the Issei the issue
was no longer what the WRA had in mind, but something
completely different: Could they face their ancestors and
their relatives in this world or in the next if they had participated in this kind of a program at all? This challenge to
the Japanese race could be met only as a group. They insisted that they had to act corporately and that anyone who
registered, regardless of his answers to those questions,
would be branded as a traitor. The WRA stuck to its guns,
insisting that no mass meeting should be held and that
everybody was expected to register by a certain date. When
it became known that the Army was also recruiting volunteers for an all-Nisei combat team, that was the straw that
broke the camel's back. A loud protest was raised against
racial segregation in the Army, not so much in defense of
the principle of racial equality as for fear that such a bat-
talion or company might very well be used for the most dangerous duties, in order to spare white men's lives. The Issei
had firmly convinced themselves that the ultimate intention
of the government was to exterminate Nisei on the battle-
field and to make the Issei men without a country.

How many hours of meetings I sat through during those explosive few weeks I cannot even begin to count. All I remember is that I did all I could to interpret the mind of the Issei
to the administration and the intention of the WRA to the
Issei. At first, both sides depended on me frantically. At the
end, neither side trusted me any more. Reason gave way to
emotion on both sides. At one of the meetings an official of
the WRA, not resident at Tule Lake, was present with an
Army officer when all the members of the executive committee of the Planning Board were given an opportunity to explain where the matter stood at Tule Lake. The chairman
of the Board frankly stated that the program was at a stand-
still. Before any of us could explain why that was so, the
visiting WRA official said (more or less), "You've been playing around with this thing long enough. We've acknowl-

edged our error and corrected it. There is no earthly reason whatsoever why you, as responsible leaders of this community, cannot persuade the people to register as required. If you cannot, that must mean there are some people in this center who are working for the Emperor of Japan and deliberately sabotaging our effort. It is up to you leaders to let us know who they are, if you cannot round them up and bring them before us." That, of course, was not the thing for him to say. I had to answer unequivocally and instantly. "If that is your attitude, sir, you might as well prepare a jail big enough to hold all of us." The meeting broke up, but we did not give up our effort to bring about some constructive result.

What Does Loyalty Mean?

The real intention of the WRA was a rather simple one. It was thought that if the public was informed that, prior to their release, all evacuees had been cleared with respect to loyalty, the major difficulty in the way of resettling the Japanese in various parts of the country would be eliminated. Like those who have been released from mental institutions with a doctor's certificate of cure, the Japanese Americans were to be trusted because they had certificates of loyalty issued by the WRA. The assumption disregarded the simple fact that such a certificate in itself made a Japanese suspect for having once been suspected of disloyalty.

Frankly, the whole program not only was based on muddled thinking, but also was executed with undue rigidity. To the WRA, loyalty was a question that every adult evacuee had to answer personally of his own free will, for to the American loyalty was an intensely personal matter. Their freedom having been taken away, the Issei in the relocation center were far from being free moral agents: they were psychologically incapable of making decisions freely any more, for they were collectively in a pathological state. Moreover, the Issei in the relocation center found himself

more and more under the spell of the cultural heritage of
Japan. In the Japanese tradition, loyalty is not a personal
matter in which one can have any sort of choice; it is predetermined for one. To be a Japanese is to be loyal to Japan,
and not to be loyal to Japan means one has never been a
Japanese. By the same token, government is to the Japanese
basically a paternalistic institution that rules the people in
the name of the emperor, who is their common father. Neither the emperor nor the government ever questions
whether a Japanese is loyal to Japan. It is assumed; no individual is required to bear the burden of thinking and deciding for himself. This collectivistic mentality had become
strong among the Issei, which made the WRA's presumably
democratic approach totally unworkable. But the WRA
stuck to its guns, persistently trying to uphold the principles
of democracy and of free choice by individuals, even when
individuality as such had ceased to exist. I must confess that
I, too, shared in this mistake. Much better results could have
been gained much more easily and quickly by a little rabble-
rousing. Harry Mayeda, Chairman of the Community Council, and I reflected on this point more than once, for we
clearly saw some possibilities, but we stubbornly rejected the
idea.

Disaffection in the Community

Next, some Issei and Kibei seized the opportunity to release their frustrations. In small groups they went around
intimidating anybody whom they judged to be pro-American, and branding them "traitors." A good friend, a Methodist minister, was beaten up; and another friend, the edi-
tor of the Japanese section of the Tule Lake newspaper, had
to have sixteen stitches in his head after an unidentified man
hit him with a lead pipe. Many Christian men and women
were subjected to all sorts of humiliation and intimidation
for some weeks, as more and more people were swayed by
the propaganda of the rabble-rousers. The Tule Lake Relo-

cation Center became a large mass of mentally unbalanced people.

In the face of such a situation, all I was able to do was to help those who stubbornly kept their faith in me not to be influenced by those half-wits terrorizing the camp with threats and vandalism. I was spared from the attack of these terrorists, thanks to a rumor for which I was not responsible —a rumor that I was an expert fencer. I was completely unaware of the danger, and continued to make my rounds of the center. The people in my block, however, were so concerned about my safety that every night a group of young men stayed in my room with me until after midnight as bodyguards. All through the night, I was told, the Division of Internal Security posted policemen around my apartment.

In the end, however, some of the ringleaders were rounded up by the internal security forces and were sent to a special camp, after which peace and order were restored. Many of the Tule Lake residents, however, still did not bother to register. The administration was again faced with a difficult decision, for, having made such a grave issue out of this program, it could not very well wink at those who had not registered. At the same time, how could they be adequately penalized? What would be punishment in keeping with the offense? What really was the nature of the offense, after all? Noncooperation in this particular program —which, objectively viewed, was both ill-conceived and mismanaged—was the extent of their offense.

Asked for our opinion, Mayeda and I told Director Coverley that the best thing was not to make another issue of the refusals. This time our recommendation was accepted, and the ill-famed incident at long last came to an end. The amazing thing was that from terrorist-ridden Tule Lake Relocation Center an appreciable number of Nisei volunteered for the all-Nisei Army unit which a couple of years later became the famed 442nd Combat Team. A movie of their story was made under the title "Go for Broke."

While we were preoccupied with the loyalty registration problem, the winter of 1943 slipped away and spring came, with thousands and thousands of geese returning from the south. One day word reached us that the Project Director was being put under considerable pressure by some citizens of a small neighboring town for having too many conscientious objectors among the school teachers at Tule Lake. This was not the first time that citizens outside the relocation center had criticized the WRA and its policies. At one time, residents of Newell, California, of Klamath Falls, Oregon, and of points even farther away, complained that while they were not getting enough meat, sugar, and cigarettes under wartime rationing, the evacuees in the camp were getting all that they wanted of everything—which of course was not true. Another time, the criticism was that the evacuees were not being put to hard enough labor, but were pampered by the all-too-soft WRA administration.

Director Coverley seriously contemplated asking all the CO's to resign their teaching positions. When Shigeo Tanabe, the Methodist minister, and I heard that, we immediately went to Mr. Coverley and stated that the CO's were our most dedicated teachers and that if they were discharged, they could hardly be replaced adequately. We advised him to stand firm and not be frightened by the voice of misguided two hundred per cent Americans. He was man enough to listen to us.

Incidents of this sort, small though they were, had a cumulative effect upon the Japanese outlook on America when taken together. The people were getting increasingly touchy, and the smallest incident tended to provoke an explosive situation. Furthermore, the distance between our community at Tule and the rest of the world, beginning with the town of Newell, had become almost insurmountable. How much easier it would have been if the barrier—yes, those fences that closed us in—had first been removed. As it was, however, those barbed-wire fences made those inside turn their faces away from those outside, while those outside were busy talking about those inside without seeing them at all. Thus, the psychological distance between them grew wider and wider as time went on.

The National Director's Visit

Not very long after the loyalty registration crisis, Dillon Myer, National Director of WRA, visited Tule Lake. In the course of his stay he held an open meeting with the public, primarily the Issei. The mess hall where the meeting took place was packed to capacity a good half-hour beforehand. One could feel the tension in the air.

Mr. Myer spoke extemporaneously and informally. Ordinarily, when interpreting, I would give, paragraph by paragraph, a résumé of what had been said in English. On this occasion I attempted to render every word into Japanese and also to convey the feeling with which it was said. Myer's speech effectively conveyed two points to the people: that he was concerned about their well-being and that he was doing his best to help them within the framework of, and through the channels established by, the WRA policy of resettlement. He made no attempt to explain away anything that had happened, and he convincingly affirmed his trust in the people.

Following his speech, the meeting was thrown open for questions. One Issei after another got up and made a long speech under the pretense of asking a question—a good old Japanese custom. For three solid hours I was on my feet interpreting back and forth, and every statement, whether couched in the polite language of the old Japanese or in the matter-of-fact language of Director Myer, was "loaded." Seldom have I thanked God more profoundly than I did that night, when the meeting ended with an exchange of words of warm appreciation and gratitude between the guest speaker and the audience.

10 Wartime America Explored

In June, 1943, I requested of the WRA, the Tule Lake administration, and the Episcopal Church, a two-month leave in order to visit the areas where the WRA was attempting to relocate Japanese people. My request met with the wholehearted approval of all parties, so toward the end of June I found myself on a bus bound for Reno, Nevada, where I was to catch the train for Denver.

My itinerary was a long and varied one, and I can still vividly recall almost every detail of it. Space, however, does not permit my enumerating all the reunions with old friends, the hospitalities accorded me by new friends and by WRA and church officials. Rather, what I shall attempt to do, after sketching my itinerary, is to present a few experiences that illuminated the whole relocation problem for me.

After first attending, with five delegates from the relocation center, the national conference of the student YMCA and YWCA at Estes Park, Colorado, I went on to visit Minneapolis; Chicago; Madison, Wisconsin; Detroit; Cleveland; Columbus; Cincinnati; St. Louis; and Kansas City, and Salina, Kansas, before returning to Tule Lake via Reno.

During most of the trip I traveled hatless and in a sport shirt. No one could have identified me on sight as a clergyman; but as a Japanese, yes. Yet at no time and in no place did I encounter any expression of hostility, suspicion, or rudeness. To be honest, I had not expected anything very bad to happen, although I would not have been astonished if there had been a few uncomfortable incidents. But there were absolutely none, and I was truly astonished.

Minneapolis

My original purpose in going to Minneapolis had been to visit the Nisei from Tule Lake who were in training at the language school at Camp Savage. However, in the course of a long interview with Mrs. Lawrence Steefel at the U.S. Employment Service office, I had my first introduction to the problem of Japanese relocation. Mrs. Steefel spent half a day, five days a week, at this office as a volunteer representing the Minneapolis Committee on Japanese American Resettlement, in which a large number of religious and civic organizations participated. She had been assigned a small room, where she interviewed Nisei applicants fresh from the relocation centers. To see men and women, both old and young, lined up in the employment agency was, I must confess, a new experience for me.

The Army had located the language school in Minneapolis after a survey had indicated the Twin Cities as having the least racial prejudice and as being the most desirable site. And there had been an earlier community committee to help make the young Nisei soldiers welcome in the Twin Cities during their leave periods. The favorable reports of these young men about their treatment aroused keen interest among the Japanese in the relocation centers who were contemplating resettlement. It was not long before the relatives, sweethearts, and friends of these soldiers were headed for the Twin Cities as a "tested" place to resettle.

It was at that point, and to meet the new problems, that

the committee which Mrs. Steefel served was organized. Its purpose was twofold: to open up employment opportunities for the resettlers and to create a social climate that made acceptance of the resettler more socially approved than rejection was. This meant hundreds of speeches by committee members before church groups, service clubs, PTA meetings, labor unions, and civic organizations. Where there were instances of express reluctance to receive the families of Nisei soldiers into neighborhoods, committee members visited the troublemakers, to reason with them. But by far the most crucial problem was employment, and the committee negotiated with the U.S. Employment Service to allow a committee member to act as the professional placement officer, on a voluntary basis, for Japanese-American applicants. Mrs. Steefel was that officer.

In the midst of our interview, a long and rather pointed telephone conversation engaged her attention. When she finished, she said to me, "In this city there are not many industries crying for skilled workers, but there are any number of middle-class families eager to employ domestic servants. The trouble is that many of them would employ the Nisei for definitely substandard wages. They justify it by saying that after all, compared with the life in the concentration camp—where, according to them, the Japanese Americans ought to be anyway—these people should be happy to get any sort of wage." So, said Mrs. Steefel, a good part of her work was to refuse job offers coming from such prospective exploiters of the evacuee labor, but to do so in such a manner that they might learn the truth about the Nisei: that they were U.S. citizens, that many of them were college graduates, and that it was not through their own fault that they had to seek new opportunities to make their living in this city. She also told me that the USES had agreed to make all files available to her, and she on her part respected the established procedure of the USES and operated strictly according to it. She and the Resettlement Committee were both opposed in principle to giving this sort of special treatment to the Nisei, but decided to do so for a limited period of time because the Nisei were coming to Minneapolis under unique circumstances over which they had had no control whatsoever.

That interview with Mrs. Steefel opened my eyes. Here was a woman of ability and status—she was the wife of a professor at the University of Minnesota and mother of two children—giving generously of her time and talents to help the Nisei coming to Minneapolis. Moreover, she did this with a firm sense of fair play and respect for the rights of all people, and with such devotion to the cause that nothing was too big to tackle or too small to attend to. And behind her stood a host of religious and civic organizations working to atone in Minnesota for the errors made in California, Oregon, and Washington. Personal confrontation with one such person actually at work profoundly affected me.

Chicago

On arriving in Chicago, I immediately visited Elmer Shirrell, who now directed the WRA office there. He informed me that on the following day there would be a semipublic meeting at the WRA office for those interested in and concerned about the problems pertaining to the resettlement of Japanese Americans. Dr. John Embree, who was to give an address, had had to cancel his trip from Washington at the last minute. Shirrell then asked me to pinch hit. Far be it for me to substitute for Dr. Embree, but the subject matter being what it was, I gladly consented to speak, and found myself sharing the platform with Dr. Robert Redfield, the world-famous professor of anthropology at the University of Chicago, whom I had had the pleasure of meeting at Tule Lake earlier. Since there was no time to prepare a formal address, I was obliged to speak extemporaneously.

One of the questions bothering the audience, to which no satisfactory answer had been given, was why the Japanese

Americans were, or at least appeared to be, so reluctant to take advantage of the WRA program. Shirrell asked me to speak on that question. My main point was that the evacuees, cooped up in the camp for so many months, had lost their perspective and could no longer distinguish what was true from what was not.

The problem, in a word, was the relocation center itself. As we discussed the problem in that conference, it became indisputably clear to me that segregation was the last method to be used in order to solve the problem of minority groups, for not only did it not solve any part of the problem, but the segregation itself became a new and larger problem than the one for which it was intended to be a solution. Segregation, whether temporary or chronic, whether marked by barbed-wire fences or merely by invisible lines of gentlemen's agreements, whether legalized by legislation or only sanctioned by social customs, results in the breakdown of communication between groups, in which both the segregated and the segregator suffer equally.

The Pioneer Hostel of the Brethren
While in Chicago I paid a visit to the Bethel Theological Seminary of the Church of the Brethren. A part of the student dormitory was then being used as the first resettlement hostel established for the benefit of the Japanese-American evacuees. Those of us who were more positively disposed to encourage the Nisei people to go out of the camp were profoundly appreciative of the imaginative step taken by the Church of the Brethren.

The hostel, directed by the Rev. Ralph Smeltzer, had as its objective two seemingly contradictory ends: protection of the Japanese-American resettlers from abuse or exploitation by the American public, and the integration of the Japanese Americans into the general stream of American life. The WRA paid the travel fare from the relocation center to the destination of the resettler's choice, plus enough money for him to live for two weeks, during which period he was expected to find both a job and a dwelling place. Frequently it was impossible to find a job within so short a time. In such a situation one's hotel bill could mount up in no time and, desperate, one could easily become a victim of exploitation. There were people who stood ready to employ intelligent and skilled Nisei for substandard wages or to offer them room and board in exchange for domestic services. There were not a few Nisei who, not knowing what sort of employment opportunity was awaiting them, came out of their camps and signed up to work as domestic servants. There was thus a situation which could have become dangerous for the future relationships between the Japanese Americans and the rest of the American community.

Another danger was the tendency of the Nisei resettlers toward what one might call self-imposed segregation. There was—or should have been—nothing wrong with this under normal circumstances, but in 1943, when American sentiment was running high against anything Japanese, it was not a very wise choice, to say the least. Although it was not entirely through any fault of their own that the Nisei had to feel like strangers in their native land, they could not afford to have white Americans point their fingers at them, saying, "See how they stay together and keep themselves apart from the rest of us. Once a Jap, always a Jap!"

The day I visited the hostel, there was an informal discussion held after dinner which I was told was a sample of many sessions regularly held there. The main part of the meeting was devoted to comparing notes and sharing experiences with regard to their job hunting and apartment searching. From time to time speakers from the WRA office, church groups, employment agencies, and other community organizations gave the prevailing picture of employment opportunities and community sentiment in the city. The hostel thus provided for those fresh out of the relocation center an excellent opportunity for orientation to the life outside. The Chicago hostel soon proved so successful that the Church of the Brethren opened a second hostel in Brooklyn; the United Lutheran Church, one in Minneapolis; the American Baptist Church, one in Cleveland; the Friends, one in Philadelphia and one in Des Moines.

I visited a number of industries that employed Japanese Americans. The one which stands out vividly in my memory was the series of farms owned and operated by the Curtiss Candy Company. At one farm were several families who had belonged to my parish in White River Valley. It was most encouraging to learn at first hand how happy they were to be earning their own living as free men again.

Other Stops in the Midwest

During my travels in Ohio, it was encouraging to learn that within the state there were several different possibilities for resettlement: Cleveland for industrial employment, the Columbus area for rural employment, Cincinnati for professional employment; and all over the state were colleges for student relocation. I was also heartened everywhere I went in Ohio to find churchmen taking a very active part in the community efforts to help the Nisei in their resettlement.

In Kansas City, Vernon Kennedy, director of the WRA regional office, was trying to open up opportunities for Japanese farmers in Missouri, Kansas, Kentucky, and the neighboring states. Complaining to me of the attitude of the Japanese farmers toward the local farming conditions, he said: "They won't go unless there's inside plumbing and electricity. What kind of farmers are they to demand such amenities? Are they really farmers?" Here I encountered for the first time the real difference in rural standards between the West Coast and the border states in the Midwest. In 1940 it was unthinkable to find farmhouses on the Pacific Coast that did not have inside plumbing and electricity. Although most of the Issei farmers had in the beginning endured much worse living conditions, they were now in no frame of mind to return to that level. Compared with it, the relocation center was a hundred times better. I at last realized why segments of the American public complained about the Japanese being pampered in the relocation centers.

My brief visit to rural Kansas convinced me that that area was no place for Japanese farmers. For one thing, farming in Missouri and Kansas was completely different from the truck gardening the Japanese were used to and known for. For another thing, the simple and otherwise good-hearted people in those states would have had a hard time accepting the Japanese people into their communities. I was convinced that they were basically good people with no animosity toward Japanese Americans because of their racial background, but I was not naïve enough to forget that they were under social pressures of all kinds, among which was the strong tendency to equate patriotism with anti-Japanese sentiment.

In late August, I arrived back at Tule Lake in good form and high spirits, to learn that the center had been officially designated a "segregation" center. It would become such as of November 1, 1943, and during the intervening two months those in Tule who had given "correct" answers to the two loyalty questions were either to leave as permanent resettlers or to be transferred to one of six relocation centers, and those in the other centers who had given "wrong" answers were to be transferred to Tule Lake.

11 The Disintegration of
Tule Lake Segregation Center

Back at Tule Lake I found that Ray Best had replaced
Harvey Coverley, who had been called to military service,
as Project Director. True to expectation, the center was
filled with tensions, and the administration was in a tight
spot. Among those who had proved their loyalty to the
United States by satisfactorily answering the form questions,
there were many, especially Issei, who resented having to be
transferred to another center, while those who had been
branded "disloyal," though in point of fact few were, were
indignant for having been so designated. Consequently, no
one was pleased with the decision made by the WRA to
make Tule Lake a segregation center, and the local administration was bearing the brunt of it all.

There was no question that the morale of the community
was at just about the lowest possible ebb. The administration had increased the staff of the relocation office in order to
accelerate the program of resettlement outside, a measure
that did not please the community at all. Furthermore, although the attempt to divide the "goats" from the "sheep"
was done "confidentially," it soon became apparent in what

category each person had been placed, and there developed an unbridgeable chasm between the two. That division turned the Tule Lake community into the most pathetic group I have ever witnessed.

The Unfairness of the Loyalty Procedure
Basically, it was a very unfair act to brand anybody as disloyal to the United States on the basis of his answer to that ill-fated questionnaire used for loyalty registration. This was especially true of the Issei, whose concepts of nation, government, and loyalty were so different from those of the American people. Their concepts, let me state emphatically, had remained Japanese chiefly because all the time they were in the United States they had been prevented by American society from becoming an integral part of it through race prejudice against them. Many Issei who declined to pledge loyalty were already past the prime of life, and as Japanese they were barred from becoming naturalized U.S. citizens. How could they, cooped up behind barbed-wire fences for more than a year, hope for any bright future for themselves in America? What would their pledge of loyalty do to help them, except to embarrass them when and if they decided to return to Japan after the war? Since the United States was not giving them their due place, they could not possibly jeopardize their chance to be accepted by their own Japan. So went their logic. The real issue was their loss of confidence in the United States government, and who could blame them for that?

In their eyes, those who had pledged their loyalty—their friends, neighbors, co-workers, and, in many instances, their relations—began to look like traitors, or at least betrayers of their confidence. Those who answered No desired, sincerely and intensely, a collective decision by all the people involved, for they had lost confidence in themselves and in their competence to make decisions on matters that would determine their personal future, as well as in their ability to

cope with wartime or postwar U.S. society. Those answering
Yes, on the other hand, desired, however hesitantly, that
each individual make his own personal decision, for they
still had some confidence in themselves. The general result
was that the former rejected the latter, however much the
latter tried to remain their friends.

The Response of the Community
To speak about resettlement in such a climate was not
very safe, let alone popular, for the antagonists were getting
more and more belligerent and vicious. Still, there were people who were curious about the world outside, if not interested in resettlement possibilities. Upon the request of such
people and with the encouragement of the administration,
I addressed an outdoor public meeting. It was an excellent
opportunity for me to report on my two months' journey.
Although I was advised not to urge people to relocate, I concluded my address with this observation:

Whatever the political or pseudo-political implications and ramifications, I have come to a firm conviction, as a result of my two
months' trip away from this center, that this is no place for anybody who wants to remain a wholesome human being. Life outside . . . is, I am sure, no picnic to anybody, but if I were asked
to choose either to vegetate in safety in the relocation center or
to live as a man by risking my personal safety in the midst of the
unknown American public, I would not hesitate to choose the
latter.

My address was food for thought for many, and bitter
medicine for others, but I had a very attentive audience;
and in the following weeks many people privately called on
me to inquire which area might be best for resettling their
respective families. On the other hand, I did not make myself popular among those who had made up their minds
never to leave the camp, unless to return to Japan. This did

not bother me at all, for every moment was filled with jobs to be done.

The first of November was the target date by which everybody who was to leave Tule Lake had to be out. In the meantime, beginning sometime in the early part of October, "segregants" from nine other centers began to be transferred in.

During those two months many human tragedies were unfolded before my eyes. Not a few families were split in two. In some families the Nisei children desired to make a new start outside, while their Issei parents were hesitant to leave the security the center offered them. In some families, mothers were so concerned over the future of their children that they were willing to take any risk to find an opportunity to restore them to normal family life outside, whereas Issei husbands and fathers were genuinely afraid that once out of the camp, they might not be able to support their families. People sought one another's advice when no one was in any position to advise the other. If only each person had thought for himself and his family, and decided what to do in view of the real situation confronting himself and his family, solutions could have been found much more simply. As it was, many people were so completely caught up in what one might call the collective frame of mind that few of them were capable of anything like independent thinking. One had always to think about what one's neighbors or friends were doing. If a majority were planning to go out of the center, one was inclined to join them; and one also felt that one should not go out if a majority were staying in the center. But how could one find out what the other was going to do when each was wondering what he was going to do? People who have lost confidence in themselves soon lose initiative, too, and become resentful toward those who confidently look after their own affairs. Pettiness, suspicion, and jealousy came to be outstanding characteristics of the Tule Lake residents.

Some Pathetic Cases

I recall several pathetic cases that I was called upon to counsel. One was that of a young man whose father had been interned by the FBI in a detention camp in New Mexico. All the members of the family were Christians. The young man and his sister were particularly active in the youth group of the Tule Lake Union Church. The family had come from a certain county in California, and the majority from that county had by then become extremely antagonistic to the WRA program. The young man wanted to leave camp and pursue his own career, but owing to his father's prolonged absence, he felt obliged to stay close to his mother and younger sisters and brothers. But now he felt the time had come for him to get out of the camp—alone, if necessary, to prepare a place for the rest of the family, but if at all possible with his mother and brothers and sisters. When this became known, his mother's friends and acquaintances began to put pressure on him to remain. Some even went so far as to say to his mother, "Your husband is in the internment camp. Certainly he will be honored by the Japanese government when the war is over. You can't afford to find yourself a traitor to your own country when your husband is receiving honor from her. Besides, under no circumstance should you cooperate with the United States government, which is keeping your husband in the internment camp. Think how he'll feel when you go out of this camp to live among our enemies." Secretly, the old woman used to come to me for counsel. Finally, against all odds, the whole family decided that they would leave. Their neighbors then made their life miserable, and even showed signs of being ready to attack and harm the young man. For several nights he came over to my room to sleep; not that my place was any safer, but at least two of us would have had a better chance to protect ourselves.

The other case involved a family split between generations. Father, mother, a boy of college age, and a high school girl constituted this family. The crux of the problem was that the young boy wanted to go to college, and the parents were afraid that once he left the camp, he would instantly be drafted into the Army. Here was a middle-aged couple, law-abiding, decent, and industrious all their lives, who had done everything in their rather limited power to provide for and educate their children, who were their only joy and hope in this world. Now their son, in his late teens, with life ahead of him, wanted to leave to go to college. If it was just a college he was going to, the parents could have reconciled themselves to it, but the thought of his being drafted was too much for them. The poor mother went nearly insane. She used to seek me out all over the camp, at any hour of the day or night, to make known her fears. The boy was determined, however, not to let his mother's emotion stand in the way of his getting a college education. When he, too, came to me to think his way through the problem, I encouraged him to disobey his parents for the time being, on the grounds that once he went away to college, his mother would accept it as *fait accompli* and would be reconciled to his decision; indeed, the day might come sooner than she thought when she would be thankful that he had stuck to his plans. Finally, the mother began to realize that her continuous nagging was doing no good. On the day of his departure, however, she got me out of bed at 3 A.M. to listen to her fears and complaints, and I kept her talking to me long enough for the boy to catch his train.

Deciding a Difficult Question

These two cases are cited here not because they were in any sense typical, but because they show the extent to which people, collectively and individually, were beside themselves. The whole community of Tule Lake was like a split personality. No one believed anyone any more. Needless to say, the administration had an awful time in dealing with the many problems that were in substance very trivial, but, in the minds of the persons involved, were magnified and intensified to life-and-death importance.

One problem that troubled many people about to be transferred was the matter of deciding to what center they should go. From the standpoint of the administration, it was just another stop before their final resettlement away from the camps; therefore, it made very little difference who went to which camp. The main point for the administration was to distribute the Tule Lakers evenly among the six camps. From the standpoint of the people, however, the center to which they were going was to be their home for the duration of the war; therefore, they felt that they had every right to choose the camp to which they were going. Objectively, one camp was just as bad or good as another, but somehow the six camps were graded among the people. People from Washington and Oregon, for example, had Minidoka, near Twin Falls, Idaho, as their first preference, for that was where most of their friends were. People from northern California wished to be transferred to Topaz, Utah, while those from central California preferred Heart Mountain, Wyoming, or Granada, Colorado. No one, irrespective of where he was originally from, wanted to be sent to the two Arkansas camps, Jerome and Rohwer. The fact that those camps were located south of the Mason-Dixon Line made them unpopular, and there were all kinds of rumors rampant about them. For example, rumor had it that they were infested with poisonous reptiles and insects and were hardly fit for human habitation, as well as being terribly humid in the long summer.

There was a great deal of resistance on the part of the internees to being transferred to a camp which they did not like. To persuade them to comply with the arrangements made by the administration was indeed one of the big jobs thrust upon its welfare department. Naturally enough, I found myself an unofficial liaison between the office of the welfare department and many disgruntled families. In several cases where reconsideration of destination was truly merited, adjustments were made.

Events Attending Departure

Prior to the departures from the center, the Rev. Dr. Clarence Gillett, ex-missionary to Japan and representative of the American Board of Foreign Missions, visited Tule Lake on behalf of the Protestant Commission. Among other items of business, he conveyed to me a message from Bishop Reifsneider, to the effect that probably I ought to stay at Tule Lake to minister to those who were going to be kept there for the duration. I begged for a few weeks in which to think over the proposal, for I felt I could not refuse it flatly— after all, those who would be coming to Tule Lake might require the ministry of the church far more than those who were eventually going to find their way back into society. Among all the Japanese clergy of all Christian denominations except the Roman Catholic, I was one of the very few then single. If somebody were to do this job, I certainly was the most suitable candidate. And to top it all, I was well known to and trusted by the local administration as well as by the national office of the WRA. Yet I was not absolutely sure whether I was the right person for the job—that is, I was very skeptical whether those Japanese who, for psychological reasons more than for any other, had turned their backs on the United States, would accept me as their pastor, counselor, and friend. On that point I indeed had at least two strikes against me in the eyes of the segregants. For that reason alone, I had to think the whole matter over very carefully.

On the last Sunday of September, 1943, a few days before the last train was to leave Tule Lake with a load of transferees, we had a large community-wide worship service at the recently finished auditorium of the Tri-State High School, with Dr. Gillett and myself as preachers. By then, many young Nisei had left Tule Lake, so I was surprised to

see the auditorium comfortably packed. I preached, on the
text "No one who puts his hand to the plow and looks back
is fit for the kingdom of God" (Luke 9:62), a hortatory sermon to urge the Nisei to stop looking back to their past and
to take a decisive step into the future. The past has a way
of taking on, in man's mind, an idealized form and appear-
ing infinitely better than it actually was. In the wilderness,
the Israelites were full of complaints and grievances against
Moses, for when they looked back to the life of bondage in
Egypt, they recalled only that they had something to eat,
however meager and scanty, every day. "Would that we had
died by the hand of the Lord in the land of Egypt, when we
sat by the fleshpots and ate bread to the full" (Exodus 16:3
RSV). I told them that as they went out of the relocation center and eventually resumed their lives in the general stream
of American society, they would undoubtedly have moments
of wondering why in heaven's name they had decided to
leave Tule Lake. Such moments might be caused by en-
countering the hostility of racially prejudiced people, by a
prolonged period of unemployment, by unsatisfying employment or housing, or even by inexplicable discouragement—things just not going right. When these moments did
come, they were bound to feel homesick for the relocation
center—not because it was a wonderful place, but chiefly
because, despite all the injustices of which it was a symbol,
it had for the past year or more given them a measure of
security and a deep sense of belonging to one another.

I went on to say:

Furthermore, many of you have found new friends with whom
you will enjoy lifetime friendship—some of you were even married while here—and for good or ill we all have had to live
a communal life pretty intensely, a communal life which was
forced upon us. There is no question whatsoever that Tule Lake
will continue to have a soft spot in your heart, and this is good.
None of us should leave this place with bitterness against it in
his heart. But beware lest this place become "fleshpot and bread

of Egypt" to you. The path of the Promised Land is always hard; it invariably includes long nights of darkness and vast areas of wilderness, but do not look back. Let the past bury the past, and press forward into the future, unknown but gloriously promising.

Dr. Gillett's sermon was based on the text "So the Lord opened the eyes of the young man, and he saw; and behold, the mountain was full of horses and chariots of fire round about Elisha" (2 Kings 6:17). It was a wonderful message of reassurance to those young Nisei as they were leaving the security of "protective custody" and venturing into the wilderness of the unknown, each intensely feeling his aloneness.

In effect, in this service, I, a young Japanese clergyman, was sending that congregation of pilgrims into American society and Clarence Gillett, one of the elder statesmen of the American Board of Foreign Missions, was there to receive them on behalf of American society.

The remaining few days of September went by more or less uneventfully. I spent many hours in the offices of the welfare services, of which Miss Saline Gifford was then chief (I was to meet her again in Geneva, Switzerland, in the late 1950's, when she came to attend the ILO conventions for two years in succession, representing the interests of "indigenous minorities" such as American Indians). There were, however, two unforgettable incidents.

On the day the train for the Jerome and Rohwer centers, the two most dreaded centers, was to leave, the military officer in charge of the sentry service at Tule Lake decided to have a minor tank unit exercise. Harry Mayeda and I laughed over the peculiar humor of the military officer; we agreed that anybody halfway intelligent would conclude from this that any place—snakes, bugs, poison ivy, and all— would be better than Tule Lake. With that observation we comforted those leaving for Arkansas. The presence of those armed tanks, however, was disquieting to me. Because Tule

Lake was becoming a segregation center, it was thought, I presume, that more rigid security measures were required. Yet those being transferred in were no more criminal or disloyal than those being transferred out. Why, then, such precaution?

The other incident was more tragicomic. The doctors had declared that an old bachelor who had been hospitalized with a light case of TB could be moved without danger, but he did not want to be transferred to any other place. Every day we tried to persuade him that it was to his own benefit, but all was in vain. The administration finally decided to leave him alone until the last moment, and then carry him into the train. Well, that moment came and an ambulance was ready, but the old fellow was nowhere to be found. Several hours of hunting did not produce him, and the train had to leave without him. Shortly thereafter he re-emerged. Everyone was impressed by his unequivocal devotion to Tule Lake, and he was finally allowed to remain.

Tule Lake as Segregation Center

The moment the last trainload of transferees left, one immediately sensed how the whole climate of Tule Lake had changed. A small group of Nisei remained, at the request of the administration, to facilitate the reception process of the incoming segregants. Harry Mayeda and I also agreed to stay through the month of October—the gray period, as it were. Tule Lake *Relocation* Center was officially closed on September 30, 1943; it reopened as *Segregation* Center on November 1.

Every few days during the month of October a new trainload of people arrived. Upon arrival they were duly processed and assigned to their living quarters. What proportion of the original Tule Lake population remained untransferred or unrelocated I do not now remember, but there must have been several thousand of them. They were there to welcome those coming from other centers, but in no time the newcomers became the dominant group, and the original group suddenly found themselves a minority barely tolerated by the new settlers. To those transferred in from the other centers, Tule Lake was the first stop on the journey back to Japan, whereas the original Tule Lakers did not feel that they had moved one step toward Japan.

I continued to occupy my old one-room apartment, and I was without any clearly defined job or responsibility. Most of my time and energy were spent as an interpreter, since communication was becoming extremely difficult. With every trainload of new arrivals, minor crises were bound to arise because at least a few families would not be satisfied with the housing arrangements arbitrarily made for them prior to their arrival.

Meeting people as they got off their train, lined up, walked from one desk to another to have all sorts of papers put in order, and finally taken to their preassigned barracks, I felt that they were a defeated people, retreating from the struggle they had been engaged in for many years, the struggle to make a go of it as immigrants to America. Each of them had his own good reason for giving up the fight, for deciding to retreat. Their being transferred to Tule Lake was the first tangible consequence of this decision.

What had happened to them? To me it was quite clear. When they were confronted by the combination of the loyalty registration under the WRA and the Army's recruitment of volunteers from among the Nisei men, they decided that it was too much for them to take and concluded that there could be no place in the United States for people of Japanese descent. Their decision to give up on the United States was neither immoral nor cowardly. I, for one, never thought ill of them because of their decision to return to Japan. (From my vantage point, it took infinitely more courage to return to wartime Japan from wartime United States. But that was another matter altogether.) I respected their decision and never doubted their integrity, knowing that each of them had to make his decision under pressure of circumstance totally unknown to me.

Still, the psychological wounds which they suffered in conceding their defeat were conspicuous in their behavior patterns. An extreme case was an old man who, when he arrived, was carrying a suitcase that appeared far too heavy for its size. Rumor eventually had it that the suitcase was filled with silver dollars, for the old man did not trust American banks or paper money, and kept all his savings in silver dollars "at home." I am sure the story was apocryphal, but, as is so often the case, a rumor like that was more indicative of the prevailing social climate than many scientifically conducted surveys or analyses could be.

Providing a Ministry for the Center

One of my concerns at this juncture was how the Christian ministry should be maintained after I left Tule Lake, for all ordained clergymen were gone by then, and there was no likelihood that anyone would be transferred in from another center, although Howard and Ruth Hannaford, then on vacation, were expected to be back on the job soon. I had been asked whether I would be willing to stay at Tule Lake as a chaplain. It was a challenge I could not dismiss lightly. I was warned, however, that if I stayed on, my life would be in danger because resentment and hostility were so intense among the people that one never knew what might happen to those who were, rightly or wrongly, identified as pro-American. I arrived at the conclusion that it is one thing to die for a cause but an entirely different thing to meet death or harm as a victim of what might be called the collective schizophrenia of a disillusioned people. So I declined the honor of remaining as chaplain.

Nevertheless, the need for professionally trained ministry was felt very keenly. I recall a married woman in her early thirties who asked for an interview with me. Her problem?

She was pregnant, but the child was not her husband's. While she was in the relocation center, boredom drove her to another man. Now she was with this unwanted child—feeling guilty for having betrayed her husband, bitterly resentful of her erstwhile lover, and deeply ashamed of herself. Since she could no longer stay where she was, she decided, under whatever pretense, to come to Tule Lake—with not the ghost of an idea where to go from there. Under the circumstances, the only thing I could do was to refer her to the Social Welfare Service.

Also unforgettable was a funeral service I conducted very shortly after Tule Lake became a segregation center. In the TB ward of the hospital was a young woman in her mid-twenties who, while working in the hospital as a nurse's aide, had contracted tuberculosis. When she died, it was my lot to officiate at her funeral service. She was not a Christian, but all the Buddhist priests had by then left the center. Word somehow spread throughout the camp that a young Christian minister was conducting a funeral service for a Buddhist girl. Curiosity must have gotten the better of many people, for the funeral service for the lonely young woman was well attended. Her untimely death would otherwise have been mourned by not more than a handful of people.

Since I had seen her a few times in the hospital and knew what sort of person she was, I had a genuine appreciation for her desire to serve others, a warm affection toward her as a person, and an admiration for the courage with which she met her death. The occasion reminded me of the death of my older half-sister during my college years in Japan. In the drab Tule Lake Center, which stood as a symbol of man's inhumanity to man, where I was daily confronted by the ugliness of human nature in all its forms, this young woman, in her death, showed me how sublime and beautiful humanity might be.

For the service I used the burial office in the Book of Common Prayer, prefacing it with the explanation that though the deceased was not a Christian, I was going to commit her soul to God, the Creator and the Preserver of all things, according to my Christian faith and conviction, for this was the only way I knew in which I could be true both to the deceased and to my Lord and Master.

The occasion called for a homily. Having read Psalm 121 (I will lift up mine eyes unto the hills) in the burial office, I referred to it in my homily, introducing it to the largely non-Christian congregation in front of me as one of the many songs which the ancient Hebrew pilgrims used to sing as they approached the city of Jerusalem, which stood upon a hill.

Pilgrimage is a common form of devotion in many religions, and Japanese Buddhism is no exception. Pilgrims' songs in the book of Psalms always remind me of the pilgrims I saw in my childhood passing through the little town where I grew up, a town located on the route which led them from one sacred place to another. The pilgrims almost always walked in groups, reciting sutras or mumbling prayers while the bells tied to their walking canes sounded monotonously but rhythmically.

The mere mention of pilgrimages was enough to capture the imagination of the old Japanese, Buddhists and Christians alike. I followed it by saying:

Human life is a pilgrimage, not walking alone, but together with others. And in the course of journeying together, all sorts of things happen to everybody—some pleasant, others painful. We grow together as men and women as we share all these experiences one with another. We are assembled here to pay tribute to this young woman, unknown though she was to most of us here, whose life was cut short while she was serving others. She was a pilgrim, as we all are. And yet, who can say that she did not live out her life to the fullest? I, for one, believe that she lived a rich life because, as I learned during the days preceding her death, she really cared for those whom she was serving. Much of her short life she lived for others, and when the time came, she faced her death with a quiet courage and a determination to keep going forward in the course of her pilgrimage.

To many men and women who came to Tule Lake disillusioned and disheartened, that funeral service provided an occasion to rethink their lives in a different light. Strange though it may sound, it can be said that the death of that unknown young woman somehow gave the emerging segregation center a chance to have a quick glimpse of sanity and serenity, which human community is capable of attaining if certain preconditions were met.

Within a few days after that unforgettable funeral service, the train from Minidoka Relocation Center in Idaho brought to the center my revered friend, Rev. Shozo Hashimoto, his wife, and his daughter. Mr. Hashimoto was the pastor of the Japanese Baptist Church in Seattle, a poet, and a recognized Biblical scholar. He and Mrs. Hashimoto decided to return to Japan solely for the sake of their daughter, then in her early teens. Evidently Mr. Hashimoto came with fear and trembling, for the prospect of life at Tule Lake was none too bright. When he saw me standing in the "reception line," he embraced me, saying repeatedly, "Oh, what a relief! Just like being met by Amida Buddha at the gate of hell." Imagine a Baptist minister saying that!

I could have said exactly the same thing to him, for he solved my big problem—namely, what to do to provide Christian ministry at Tule Lake after November 1, 1943. What a relief it was to me, to see my highly esteemed friend Hashimoto there! Moreover, there were, both among those who stayed on at Tule Lake and among those who were transferred there from other centers, a small number of firmly committed Christian people. I was profoundly grateful to have the assurance that there would be at Tule Lake a nucleus of Christians with an excellent pastor to lead them.

Why did I think it was going to be so hard to minister to

the people at Tule Lake? There were signs that foretold what was to come. One was the sudden increase of vandalism—a totally senseless kind of vandalism. One night a group of Kibei young men who had just arrived from another center piled up chairs from the school building and made a bonfire of them. Another day, as we were trying to help a group of new arrivals to get settled, Kibei youth incessantly made a nuisance of themselves by making silly remarks in Japanese to the Nisei and Caucasian staff. I lost my temper with them and, to everybody's utter astonishment, told them off in Japanese: "You're trying to demonstrate how patriotic you are to Japan by refusing to use English. But in fact, being Kibei, you don't have too good a command of English. What a disgrace you are to Japan, making such a shameful scene in front of Americans."

Corliss Carter, who was standing by me, said, "My gosh, I don't know what you said, but it sounded like pretty strong language you were pouring on those poor devils!"

Clear Signs of Disintegration
There was another activity indicative of the prevailing state of mind. At one of the recreation halls, a group of men put up a sign in Japanese to publicize a "training school" for youths wishing to become fighters for the achievement of the "Great East Asia Co-Prosperity," under the aggressive military leadership of imperial Japan. Every morning they assembled youngsters for setting-up exercises. But they also kept them from attending the "public" schools in the center, proposing to teach the youngsters whose parents so wished all subjects in the Japanese language. How long this was tolerated by the administration after I left, I do not know, but that is immaterial. What is important is that people resorted to this kind of action primarily to register their disappointment with and protest against the government, and to express their desperate need to identify themselves as

Japanese in order to compensate for the bitter defeat they had suffered in America.

To them the segregation center was a wonderful asylum, a little island apart from society, something of a little Japan, where they could dream of an idealized Japan, undisturbed by the cold facts of life or the bitter reality of history. It was a terrible thing to subject children to, children who had no other choice but to accompany their parents. Not all the adults lost touch with reality, but once in that center most of them did not escape being affected by its pathological atmosphere.

It was really sad to see many otherwise sane and healthy people go to pieces like this—not so much individually as collectively. Morally, none of them had anything to be blamed for. They were no different from those who had answered Yes on their questionnaires, except that in their own minds they felt that they had been completely defeated and that the only recourse left for them was to return to Japan. They rejected America because they felt America had rejected them.

This sociopsychological context would make it almost impossible, I concluded, for the minister to reach the very people who desperately needed his help. At stake was not only the "salvation" of these wretched people, but also that of the United States itself. One could not be attained without the other, and the two could only be attained together, when the alienated Japanese became reconciled to the America that had alienated them.

I was not really glad when I left Tule Lake—not that I felt guilty, but somehow I was terribly sorry that I could not remain there to attempt at least being a friend to those who felt so friendless in that dreary, dismal place with violence in the air.

12 Odyssey of Re-entry

On October 31, 1943, Harry Mayeda and I left Tule Lake. The decision of Harry's parents and younger brother to remain at Tule Lake was hard on Harry, but at that moment nothing could be done about it. The day before our departure, a rumor reached Harry that hoodlums planned to attack him during the night. Since it was no time to take chances, he spent the night in my quarters. Trusting the security crew on duty and fatigued from many days' overwork, both of us slept soundly. In the morning, Howard and Ruth Hannaford kindly drove us to Klamath Falls, where we boarded a bus for Minidoka Relocation Center in Idaho.

On leaving Tule Lake, Harry and I shared the same difficult problem: neither knew where he wanted to go. We were absolutely sure that we did not want to be transferred to another relocation center—we had had enough of that at Tule Lake. Furthermore, regardless of where we might go, we would really have no time to look for a job, because the WRA regulation provided only railway fare to one's destination and living expenses for two weeks. We finally chose Cincinnati, Ohio, as our destination, simply because it was the farthest point east the WRA could send us at the time.

Our Visit to the Relocation Centers

Having set Cincinnati as our destination, we suggested to the WRA that if it would be of interest to them to find out how the Tule Lakers transferred to six relocation centers were faring, we would gladly visit those centers en route to Cincinnati, and report. To our happy surprise, the WRA enthusiastically approved our proposal.

In spite of the hostile climate at Tule Lake, a large group of well-wishers assembled at the gate to see us off. Many friends sighed with relief that we were leaving Tule Lake before it was too late. For a number of older folk it was a tearful parting, and indeed, I have not seen most of them since. Again I paused to look up at the rocky, treeless hill standing majestically against the clear blue sky, the hill which had never failed to uplift my spirit amid all vicissitudes. As the car driven by Howard Hannaford went through the gate, I found myself repeating, "I will lift up mine eyes unto the hills; from whence cometh my help? My help cometh even from the Lord, who has made heaven and earth." So my life at Tule Lake began and ended with Psalm 121 on my lips.

Harry and I decided to visit the center at Minidoka, Idaho, first; then those at Topaz, Utah; Granada, Colorado; and, finally, Jerome and Rohwer, Arkansas. We omitted Heart Mountain, Wyoming, from our itinerary purely for geographical reasons. We planned to stay at each relocation center two or three nights, to use night trains for the long hauls, and to complete our visits in three weeks.

During our journey, Mayeda and I shared what hundreds of Nisei and Issei experienced during those years of resettlement. Leaving the relocation center was to them nothing short of a journey of re-entry into American society. Life in the relocation center was virtually like living in a foreign country, though by no means like living in a prison. Sometime earlier my friend Shigeo Tanabe had, in a letter to the editors of *Christian Century,* pointed out how effective an institution of de-Americanization a relocation center proved to be.

In this respect, I found myself less handicapped than most of the Nisei, in spite of the fact that I was legally an enemy national, while they were native-born citizens, and that my English was a foreigner's English, while theirs was their first language. I had, moreover, other advantages. While their firsthand experience of life in the United States was generally limited to that of the Pacific Coast states, I had lived in New York and had traveled in Europe as well as extensively in this country. More recently I had taken a two-month-long trip of observation and exploration. In short, I, a foreigner, had studied, because I had to, American society, the American people, and their way of thinking, which most Nisei, as native Americans, had never really done.

The point was brought home, before we reached Minidoka Center, by Harry's remarks about the way I conducted myself. As our bus rolled out of Klamath Falls, I took out the latest issue of the *Anglican Theological Review* to read a long article by Paul Tillich. After a while, however, the physical fatigue which had accumulated over the past several weeks took hold of me, and I fell asleep. When I awakened, Harry told me that both the civilians and the military personnel who had gotten on or off the bus had looked at us with great curiosity, an action that had made him not a little nervous. I judged his reaction to be a good example of what racial segregation does to an individual. If a man of Harry Mayeda's calibre and background—he was a graduate of the University of California and San Francisco Law School, and had been a practicing attorney—was thus affected, how much more so would be the rank and file of Nisei, not to mention the Issei. After a substantial period of life behind barbed-wire fences, we all needed to be oriented once more to American life.

Tillich's article, "Storms of Our Time," which I began to read on the bus, affected me profoundly; and the reading of it turned out to be providential. I literally devoured it, paragraph after paragraph, as if it had been written solely for my own benefit, to explain why I was where I was and doing what I was then doing.

The present world war is a part of a world revolution . . . The very fact that world wars are possible and that they have become the only possible form of war shows a fundamental change from all former periods of history. Something has come into existence which never had existed before: world as a historical reality! . . . We must become actually what we have become potentially: a "world."

The substance of that paragraph has remained with me all these years and has helped me to maintain perspective as I deal with problems of race relations in America, and with Christian responsibility in areas of rapid social change in Africa, Asia, and other areas.

Tillich's thesis transformed me from one of the victims of misfortune, whether caused by the wartime hysteria of the American people, by the collective folly of the government in coping with it, or by the deliberate devices of highly organized interest groups, to one of the participants in contemporary history, moving toward a universal society. What better orientation to life in American society could I have had than that which Tillich offered me?

The few days we spent at the Minidoka Center gave us a chance to renew old friendships with Tule Lake people as well as those from Seattle. In all quarters we received a royal welcome. It was noted that the ex-Tule Lakers, although politely received at Minidoka, did not feel truly welcome. This was quite understandable, for they had come from a highly ingrown community, with a strong in-group mentality, to another equally ingrown community. At the same time, their arrival as a new, somewhat alien, group had infused fresh blood into a community that was already slowly deteriorating from boredom.

While at Minidoka we heard about the riot at Tule Lake, which shook the WRA and every Japanese community in the country: a Caucasian doctor had been bodily attacked in the hospital and the Japanese manager of the Co-op Store had been murdered. What might have happened to Harry and me had we stayed on for another week was purely a matter of conjecture, but chances were that we could not have escaped unpleasant, if not dire, consequence.

At Topaz we renewed friendships with those who had come there from Tule Lake, and for the first time I met a good number of people from San Francisco and the Bay area. From Topaz we went to Granada, Colorado, and then to Jerome and Rohwer, Arkansas. As we visited one center after another, we became more and more impressed with the ingenuity of the government in finding such uniformly God-forsaken places for relocation centers. At all these centers a substantial amount of land had been reclaimed by the industrious efforts of the Japanese internees. It was also of interest to us that the two Arkansas centers which had been most dreaded by the people at Tule Lake as the worst of all the centers, turned out to be the most pleasant ones. They were the only centers with many tall trees within the enclosures, and the Arkansas climate in November was very pleasant. Such a situation was a far cry from treeless Tule Lake in the midst of a sea of sagebrush.

We found former Tule Lakers in the five relocation centers healthy and in good humor, though not entirely without problems of adjustment and of acceptance by the older center residents. Our visit to each center seemed to boost morale and, indirectly, to help the Tule Lakers in making their adjustment.

What We Reported

When our assignment was over, I discovered that what I had observed made an interesting comparative study of the ethos prevailing in each place. For example, the Minidoka community, which was made up chiefly of city folk from Seattle and Portland were, by November, 1943, beginning to show signs of being content to remain there for the duration. There was no evidence of revolt on the part of anybody against anything. Most of the college-age youths had already departed, either for student relocation or for permanent resettlement. This was quite understandable, because the Nisei from the Pacific Northwest had been, relatively speaking, better integrated into American society than those from other sections; and consequently, when the WRA encouraged permanent resettlement, most of those eligible took advantage of the offer. Many also volunteered to serve in the all-Nisei combat unit, later to become famous as the 442nd Combat Regiment. Thus, at the time of our visit the Nisei population of Minidoka was mostly teenagers or younger children. Because the Issei were mostly city folk, it was extremely difficult to find jobs for them comparable to what they had had without making sizable capital available to them. The majority of them were not physically equal to farm work, so the Issei had pretty much given up the idea of relocating outside for the time being and were content to vegetate in the camp. In view of the situation, it was natural that the arrival of a large number of ex-Tule Lakers was resented, for it disturbed the complacency of the community.

We found similar resentment at Topaz, the ex-Tule Lakers being openly treated as a minority group. Harry and I were told that the old Topaz residents often said, whenever anything unsavory happened in the center, "Before the people of Tule Lake came, nothing like this happened here." It was noticed here, too, that those who had not gone out to resettle by then were more or less passive types, biding their time. All this meant that the longer these people stayed in the relocation center, the more unprepared they would be for entering normal society.

At Granada we had the good fortune of walking into a

conference of the relocation committee of that center. The issue confronting the committee was the widespread passive resistance there to the WRA relocation program. The internees just would not move. The community analyst, on the basis of a study, listed five things that deterred people: (1) uncertainty about whether they would be accepted in a new community; (2) uncertainty about the outcome of the war; (3) resistance as an expression of protest against the government for the way they had been treated; (4) unwillingness to assume the financial insecurity involved in resettlement; (5) complacency and the false sense of security which the center gave them. By then these people had almost convinced themselves of the rightness of "protective custody." The WRA propaganda, publicity, and promotion were reaching only those already dissatisfied with their life of confinement and those ready for adventure.

At the two Arkansas centers, Jerome and Rohwer, we learned that the inmates had always thought of Tule Lake as the most marvelous center of all. We could not help wondering what was behind this image-building of centers other than the one in which the people were residing. One thing was clear to me—that the longer these people lived in confinement, the more gullible and wishful they became about things beyond their reach, and the more they disbelieved what they did not want to believe. This tendency was universal in the centers.

At Jerome and Rohwer there were also widespread fear of informers among the residents and a general climate of suspicion and oppressiveness. Not that the administrative staff were unfriendly or inaccessible to the internees, but the internees' attitude toward the administration tended to be that of wooing favor, instead of working with it to solve common problems.

At all the centers, the arrival of transferees from Tule Lake had given the residents the false impression that the WRA intended to operate the relocation centers for a long time to come, in spite of the explicit repeated statements to the contrary. On the other hand, from the standpoint of the American people then being encouraged to receive internees into their midst, the WRA policy was loaded with inconsistency: "If they are good enough to come to our community, why aren't these Japanese allowed to go back to where they belong? If they are not acceptable to California, Oregon, and Washington, why should they be here? There must be reasons which make them undesirable." It was to alleviate the fear on the part of the American public that the WRA adopted the policy of highly individualized relocation.

At this point the WRA failed to take two vitally important steps: (1) to inform the residents of the centers decisively and even harshly that the WRA had plans to liquidate all centers in the near future; (2) at the same time, to help the residents to see that, regardless of the WRA policy, it was to their own benefit to relocate outside, because life within the centers was becoming morally deteriorating. Already something akin to the "ghetto mentality" of Negro Americans or the "reservation mentality" of American Indians was to be observed among Japanese Americans who had spent only eighteen to twenty months in confinement.

Such a program should have been at the heart of the church's work with the people still in the centers, but I am not sure whether the clergy who were in the same plight as their people were aware of this. At any rate, little did I dream then that for the following year I would be engaged in just that sort of work on a more or less nation-wide basis.

On to New York and a New Assignment

Harry Mayeda and I finally arrived in Cincinnati on November 20, 1943. There a letter was awaiting me from Dr. George Wieland, of the National Council of the Episcopal Church, suggesting that I come to New York to discuss my future work. So, within a few days, having obtained

clearance from the U.S. Attorney's office to enter the Eastern
Defense Command, Harry and I were on our way to New
York. There we were given accommodations at Pintard Hall
by my alma mater, General Theological Seminary. I pro-
ceeded to make my appointments and to visit old friends.
Meanwhile, Harry set out to explore job opportunities.

At my meeting with Dr. Wieland and Bishop Reifsneider,
it was proposed that I serve as a field secretary with the Committee on Japanese American Resettlement of the Federal
Council of Churches. I gladly accepted, and almost immediately I found myself with an assignment to explore the
possibilities for Japanese-American relocation in the Boston
area.

While in New York I had two other interviews of special
significance for the work I was about to undertake. The first
was with the Rev. Alfred Akamatsu of the Methodist Church
and Dr. Hachiro Yuasa, who later became president of
Japan International Christian University. Our discussion
concerned whether Japanese-American and Issei Christians
should be organized into their own congregations or integrated into existing churches. It was in the course of this
discussion that I saw, for the first time, that the issue had
to be dealt with, by both the church and American society
as a whole, not on an interpersonal basis, but corporately,
on an intergroup basis; that the basic problems arose because of what race stood for in the mind of the general public and because of what people thought race was.

The second interview which was to prove most helpful
was one with the Rev. Dr. Almon Pepper, who directed my
attention to the importance of working with professional
social work agencies. Over against the purely individualistic
approach to the problem of resettling people, he convinced
me of the need of an organized approach that would utilize
the resources and skills of professional agencies, both public
and private.

During this period I also learned that employment and

housing were not the only problems confronting those from the relocation centers who were trying to re-establish themselves in society. Among other problems, the reunification of families was a pressing issue for many. It was one thing for a Nisei college graduate to find employment; it was quite a different matter for him to prepare a place for his parents and his younger brothers and sisters, all of whom suddenly became his dependents. Moreover, the moment one began to move from resettlement of individuals to that of family units, one had to include in one's thinking the aging, the invalid, the minors, and the otherwise unemployable. Japanese-American resettlement was just then entering into this phase, and Dr. Pepper's counsel was of enormous help to me.

A Visit to Boston

In early December I went to Boston, where I had a most encouraging and helpful interview with Bishop Henry Knox Sherrill. In addition to acquainting me with the general situation and placing certain facilities at my disposal, he personally made appointments for me with influential citizens who could be helpful in opening up job opportunities for relocatees. I also discovered that a group of social agencies was already working with WRA on resettlement.

Thanks to the efforts of these dedicated people, both professional and volunteer, I met a number of Nisei and some Issei who had recently been brought from relocation centers. By and large they were doing fairly well, although most of them, especially Issei, were feeling desperately lonely. This was quite understandable. Anybody born and reared on the West Coast is likely to have difficulty adjusting to New England in terms of social as well as natural climate. For those who had grown up in racially segregated society and then spent a year or more in a relocation center, it was doubly difficult. Local citizens were very much aware of the problem and were doing their best to overcome it.

During my stay, the Rev. Gardiner Day invited me to preach at Christ Church, Cambridge, at the two morning services. At both services there were many servicemen. When introducing me to the congregation, Mr. Day said, "I want you to meet Mr. Kitagawa after the service and learn that Japanese people are not all such as we have been made to believe them to be by our wartime propaganda." I preached on the God-given unity of all mankind, as emphasized in the teaching of Jesus.

After the service, among the many people who came forward to greet me was a young Marine, who said, "Father, I, too, believe what you said in your sermon is absolutely true. I'm glad that I was in the church this morning to hear you preach that particular message." He paused for a little while, then continued, "I was training as a violinist, but that's all finished, for in the South Pacific my right wrist was permanently injured by shrapnel. When I was discharged, I vowed to kill the first Japanese I met. You know, Father, you're that Japanese!" Having said this, he extended his injured hand to me. I still wonder what has become of Stanley Spector, that young Marine. He demonstrated to me the power of forgiveness and reconciliation that God gives to those who in faith are willing to accept it.

Some Special Assignments

Subsequent to my visit to Boston, my field work assignments took me to many parts of the country. In many places, in addition to studying local relocation possibilities, I renewed old and valued friendships. I also attended an important meeting of the Christian churches in Denver, at which the future mission and ministry to people of Japanese descent was discussed.

After the Denver meeting I had the opportunity of visiting the Heart Mountain Relocation Center in Wyoming. There it was interesting to note that while the relocation program was in disrepute, curiosity about the world outside was increasing among the internees. Mothers, in particular, were becoming intensely concerned about the lasting impact of camp life upon their growing children and were positively eager to resettle, while the men continued to be stubbornly reluctant. Their Japanese sense of pride would not allow the men to venture into the unknown, lest by failing they should make fools of themselves. Not a few men in this predicament sought me out for confidential talks. They did not want their neighbors or, in some instances, their wives to know that they were breaking down in their resistance to the WRA policy of relocation. This was also a matter of face-saving as far as their acquaintances and relatives were concerned. These men were really agonized souls, not knowing where to turn in the face of the mounting tensions between themselves and their wives over the welfare of their children.

One of my joys at the center was to report how the young Nisei generally were doing outside and, in some cases, to report to parents about their sons and daughters on the basis of personal observation. Some parents, I am sure, were expecting to hear that their daughters had been molested or that their sons had been beaten by hoodlums.

My talks with the Rev. Gyomei Kubose, the Buddhist priest, and his young assistant were very helpful and illuminating. It was Rev. Kubose's opinion that a majority of the people he knew were secretly waiting for WRA to present concrete relocation plans—that is, to offer definite jobs in a specific community. He advocated that WRA develop a group relocation program where several families would go out as a unit to the same community. Such a program would indeed overcome the fears and uncertainties of many who were hesitant about leaving.

On leaving Heart Mountain, I undertook to investigate the Tri-County Irrigation Project in central Nebraska as a relocation possibility for farmers. As my technical consultant, I had with me Charles Furuta, a young farmer from Kent. En route to Nebraska, we investigated another relocation possibility in Hardin, Montana, and recommended that it be considered as a resettlement area for twenty-five families.

In our investigation of the Tri-County Irrigation Project, I attempted to assess the sociological situation and the attitudes in the communities toward people of Japanese descent, while Charles evaluated soil, crops, weather conditions, and so on. On completing our investigation, we recommended the Project as a resettlement possibility for a limited number of farmers, pointing out, however, that the first few years might be a time of some hardship and would demand patience on the part of the settlers.

During the first half of 1944, I made other tours of investigation, the details of which I shall not recount here. In my last report to the Federal Council of Churches' Committee on Resettlement, I attempted to summarize the positive and negative features in the general farm situation which I had observed.

On the positive side, I had not observed organized opposition to Japanese-American resettlement, although there were still pockets of prejudice and resentment. "No Japs" signs, for example, appeared principally in barber shops and restaurants, but stores generally accorded Japanese Americans courteous service. One crying need of relocatees and seasonal workers, I pointed out, was for adequate recreational facilities, little being open to them except the movies. The report also noted that farm owners tended to welcome Japanese farmers, while tenant farmers tended to oppose their entry into a community because they feared competition. With respect to undertaking seasonal work, I emphasized the importance of sending the men out in crews under a leader who would act as spokesman, a precaution necessary to prevent exploitation. I also noted that with many young Japanese Americans entering the armed forces under the

Selective Service Act, a program for the care of their wives and children required immediate attention.

My last weeks as a field secretary were spent largely in the New York area, and on July 1, I left for Chicago to marry Miss Fujiko Sugimoto, a young lady whom I had met on my visit to Heidelberg College, in Ohio.

My New Life in Minneapolis

At the reception following my marriage, Dr. George Wieland told me that I was next to be assigned to work in Minnesota, primarily with Nisei soldiers training at Camp Savage. This was indeed astonishing news to me. How could I, a Japanese national (and therefore an enemy alien), be assigned to work with U.S. Army personnel?

The story was this. Camp Savage had, of course, army chaplains on duty, as did every other Army establishment. But the commandant of the Military Intelligence Service Language School (MISLS) wanted my services because he was aware that some of the problems bothering the Nisei soldiers under his command required firsthand knowledge not only of their Japanese cultural heritage but also of the collective mentality then prevalent in the relocation centers.

As late as summer of 1944, most Nisei at Camp Savage had parents, brothers and sisters, or other relatives still in the relocation centers. The parents of many were exceedingly unhappy, in fact profoundly disturbed, to see their sons wearing the U.S. uniform and, of all things, being trained as "spies" (as they thought of the intelligence service) against their own country, Japan. In various ways parents and the elders in the relocation centers were attempting to dissuade the Nisei from pursuing their training.

To see one's aging parents go to pieces is painful to anyone under any circumstances. To the Nisei youth in military service who was destined to be sent to the Pacific to fight the imperialist Japanese and to use the knowledge of the

Japanese language as his weapon, as it were, it was an unbearable situation. He could not help feeling that he was
the cause of his aging and already helpless parents' emotional torture. The issue was a conflict of loyalties: loyalty
to one's nation versus loyalty to one's parents. For the Nisei
both loyalties were intense, and they suffered deeply from
the inevitable conflict between the two. This inner conflict
could not but show in their morale.

The commandant of Camp Savage and the Personnel
Procurement Officer, then Col. Kai Rasmussen and First Lt.
Paul F. Rusch, respectively, determined to meet this problem of Nisei morale, turned to the Episcopal Church with
the proposition that I be stationed in Minneapolis for a few
years. My specific assignment was to be an unofficial civilian
chaplain to the Nisei soldiers at the MISLS, then based at
Camp Savage and soon to be moved to Fort Snelling.

My wife and I arrived in Minneapolis on July 31, 1944,
in the midst of its annual Aquatennial Festival. Staying at
the King Cole Hotel, adjacent to Loring Park, I started
work with the Minneapolis Church Federation (later known
as the Greater Minneapolis Council of Churches), under
the Rev. Howard Wiley, Executive Secretary, while my wife
kept herself busy apartment hunting. As a newlywed couple,
we had our share of woes and problems of resettlement in a
strange city.

The first thing I had to do, being an enemy alien, was to
report to the U.S. Attorney's office in St. Paul to obtain a
permit to travel. Technically, I had to have a permit each
time I went out of Minneapolis. Foreseeing that the resettling Nisei and Issei were going to be widely dispersed in different parts of the state, I asked the District Attorney for a
blanket permit to cover the entire state of Minnesota. Such
a permit was granted, subject to renewal every three months.
I was cautioned that military establishments such as Camp
Savage and Fort Snelling were outside the District Attorney's

jurisdiction and that I needed a special permit to cover them.

Next, accompanied by my old friend and teacher, Lt. Rusch, I went to see Col. Rasmussen. A naturalized citizen of Danish origin and an accomplished linguist—besides several European languages, he also spoke Japanese—Col. Rasmussen had a profound respect and love for the Japanese culture and people. He said to me, "My soldiers need your ministry. Regard this school as your parish. Come here any time of the day or night, as need arises. Be a friend and pastor to my men." He then told me that the same arrangement would stand when the school moved to Fort Snelling.

The third thing I had to do was to report to the Bishop of Minnesota, the Rt. Rev. Stephen E. Keeler, who welcomed me to his diocese and gave me his blessing to work as a staff member of the Minneapolis Church Federation. Shortly thereafter I established a working relationship with the St. Paul Council of Churches.

While the stage was now set for my work, the finding of suitable housing was another matter. It took us a good two weeks before we found a tiny three-room house at the north end of Minneapolis. The man who showed us the house was not a realtor, but a private citizen acting on behalf of his sister, who was then living in Florida. The house was on a corner lot in a quiet residential section, a couple blocks from the end of one of the streetcar lines.

We liked the house, and the man seemed to like us. We paid the first month's rent then and there, and with a deep sigh of relief at having at last found a house to live in after two weeks' intensive search, we went back to the hotel to rest. Almost immediately after our arrival the telephone rang, and the man who had just rented us the house informed me that he had changed his mind because there was opposition from neighbors.

In answer I said, "We haven't seen any of the neighbors

yet, nor have they met us. How do they know that we're objectionable to them? I believe it's just the matter of getting to know one another, and we're prepared to go more than halfway. Just give us a few days in that neighborhood, and if, after knowing us, they still object, then we'll move out." The man agreed to let us move into the house.

In another half hour he was on the phone again, to tell us that the pressure was becoming unbearable and to beg us to reconsider. This time I decided to use a different tack and insisted that he and, for that matter, those who were objecting should go and see my bishop to find out what sort of people we were and why we had come to Minneapolis. That evening he called to tell us that he had talked with Bishop Keeler and had reported the whole thing to his sister by phone, and that she was pleased to rent us her house. We never did learn who had so intimidated that man.

The day we moved into our new home, my wife went to the corner grocery store and came back with several neighborhood children helping her carry her groceries. In no time we got to know our neighbors—the Hansens, Quams, McClellans, Lynches, Engbergs, and Engstroms. We lived in that little house for five years, and when our first child was born, the whole neighborhood shared in our joy.

Our new life had begun.

Epilogue

Those internment years were, thank God, only a few years in the nation's history, but they were a period of intense suffering for a person of Japanese descent. In terms of his personal life, those years constitute an enormously significant span. To me they represent the experience of several generations telescoped into a few months. I feel as if I had lived several men's lives during those years and, amazingly enough, even managed to take them in stride—although I would never choose to repeat them.

I have no intention of engaging in any eyewashing with respect to the compulsory mass evacuation of people of Japanese descent from the Pacific Coast in 1942. I still maintain, as I then believed, that it was neither right nor necessary. That unexpectedly good things came out of it cannot make it good, let alone right. The irreparable economic loss suffered was not the only injustice inflicted upon those involved. The far greater injustice was the fact that, with no charge against them save that of being of Japanese descent, they were forced to leave their homes and the localities where they had been law-abiding, tax-paying citizens—at the very time when the United States was fighting Hitler's racism in Europe.

One must never forget, furthermore, that that infamous move took place by order of the federal government, at a period when the civil courts were functioning normally. It was not the deed of a bunch of hoodlums or of local vigilantes, nor was it done while martial law was in force. To make the matter even worse, the forced internment of the Issei and Nisei en masse was later declared constitutionally justifiable by the Supreme Court. And, be it noted, that ruling remains on the books, unchanged.

Having said all this, let me state publicly that the experience nevertheless enriched my personal life as nothing else could have, and I venture to think that a great number of Issei and Nisei, especially Nisei, feel the same way. It is my humble and sincere hope, however, that this nation would be wiser today than to commit so stupendous a mistake by official act, especially when dealing with the complex problems of the integration of racial and ethnic minorities, the treatment of political dissenters, and the participation of the dispossessed masses in self-help programs. The mass evacuation and the forced internment of people of Japanese descent, while intended to solve a problem, in reality created a series of new problems that were much worse. Internment is an extreme form of segregation, and the experience of Japanese and Japanese Americans has conclusively proved how ineffective a means segregation is in solving the problems of a group believed to be a *problem people*. We are left with no doubt that the cleverness of man is decidedly not as wise as the foolishness of God, to borrow the classic expression of St. Paul.

One learns from this that wherever a group of people is believed to be a problem people, one had better suspect that the problem may very well lie with the part of the society that so believes. The white man, for example, who looks upon every black man as a "white man's burden," by virtue of that very fact is more than likely himself the "black man's burden." A society that refuses to accept heterogeneous groups, presumably out of an interest in peace and order or for reasons of homogeneity, is not helped by being allowed to segregate all those whom it regards as undesirable. It makes no difference whether they are racial or ethnic minorities, language groups, migrant workers, economically indigent or dispossessed people, or political dissenters— segregating them usually turns them into collective images, and as such they are more likely to haunt that society and pathologically preoccupy the mind of those who have rejected them. Forced segregation does not result in the proverbial "Out of sight, out of mind." On the contrary, the apocryphal story of mistranslation by a computer of this proverb as "blind and mad" rings true as an indication of the stupidity at work. It is nothing less than blindness and madness to think that by segregating those regarded as undesirable, society can conveniently forget them. The problem will always be intensified.

Related to this is the fact that segregation gives birth to ghetto mentality, both in the segregated and in the segregators. It is the ghetto mentality, and not so much the racial prejudice per se, that menaces our society. Furthermore, nothing is more tenacious than ghetto mentality, once it comes into being. It is impossible to demolish it without first destroying the segregation. The other way 'round never works. Those who still hold that by changing the hearts of individuals through education and persuasion alone the whole society will eventually be free from racial prejudice and discrimination, are greatly mistaken. For how can one love, respect, and relate oneself to those who are nothing but samples of a group image? Without opportunities to see, hear, and associate with those whose collective image haunts one, one can hardly be liberated from that image.

Hence, desegration is a necessary precondition for, or the first step toward, a truly integrated society, which alone liberates its citizens from the various forms of ghetto mentality.

Finally, it was through personal encounters with innumerable Americans from widely different walks of life in many parts of the nation, often in potentially explosive situations, that I came to realize the greatness of this country. This greatness does not rest in military strength, material wealth, or even political structures, but in the American people, the majority of whom are willing and able to face the unknown with open mind and in a spirit of exploration and experimentation. I am not blind to the fact that there are people, in high and low places, in politics, industry, and private sectors of society, whose minds are closed and who, therefore, easily panic before any sort of crisis or unfamiliar situation. These people can be, and have often proved to be, nasty to those whom they do not like, and go to any extent to keep them from sharing in the benefits of this great nation. My wartime experience of the American people, which was both intensive and extensive, convinced me, however, that such narrow-minded and bigoted people are definitely in the minority. But of equal importance is the fact that, though few in number, they exert tremendous influence because they are determined, vocal, and highly organized.

The most precious lesson I learned from my internment years is how desperately important it is for American society to strengthen the moral fiber and the backbone of the fair and open-minded majority so that it will not be trampled by any vocally gifted, vicious minority. America is a democratic society in which truly democratic people can easily be victimized by a determined minority of decidedly antidemocratic philosophy. How to protect America from being so preyed upon by one or another of these antidemocratic forces remains a worthy challenge to the American people. It is profoundly hoped that thoughtful reflection on the bitter experience of Issei and Nisei during the years of their forced internment may help the American people to understand this problem.

Author's Note

To those interested in pursuing scholarly studies on various aspects of the issues dealt with in this volume, the following books are recommended. The War Relocation Authority published a series of official reports (Washington: Government Printing Office, 1943-46):

Wartime Exile: The Exclusion of the Japanese American from the West Coast

The Evacuated People

The Wartime Handling of Evacuee Property

Token Shipment: The Story of America's War Refugee Shelter

Legal and Constitutional Phases of the W.R.A. Program

Community Government in War Relocation Centers

Administrative Highlights of the W.R.A. Program

People in Motion: The Post-War Adjustment of the Evacuated Japanese American

For study from a legal and constitutional point of view, the definitive volume is Morton Grodzin's *Americans Betrayed* (University of Chicago Press, 1949). For those primarily interested in sociological study on the subject, the following twin volumes are indispensable. Dorothy S. Thomas and Richard Nishimoto, *The Spoilage* (Berkeley: University of California Press, 1946) and Dorothy S. Thomas with Charles Kikuchi and James Sakoda, *The Salvage* (University of California Press, 1952). A more psychologically oriented analysis of one of the relocation centers is Alexander H. Leighton's *The Governing of Man* (Princeton, N.J.: Princeton University Press, 1945).

Carey McWilliams' *Prejudice; Japanese Americans: Symbol of Racial Intolerance* (Boston: Little, Brown, 1944) is an indispensable study, based on historical and economic analyses, of interracial tensions on the Pacific Coast which culminated in the mass evacuation of the Japanese Americans. His *Brothers Under the Skin* (Boston: Little, Brown, 1942; revised 1951) provides an excellent background.

To convey the pathos of the Japanese Americans during their internment years, none excels Minè Okubo's *Citizen 13660* (New York: Columbia University Press, 1946; reprinted by AMS Press, 1967), a book of sketches and brief comments by a sensitive young Nisei artist.

For a readable history of Japanese immigration to the United States, Bradford Smith's *Americans from Japan* (Philadelphia: J. B. Lippincott, 1948) is highly recommended.